Black Gold in Paradise

RECLAIMING SIGNAL HILL

A DEVELOPMENT HISTORY

KEN FARFSING

Signal Hill City Manager
July 1996 – June 2015

*Sam
Thanks for your
love & support!
Dad   4/26/20*

Black Gold in Paradise: Reclaiming Signal Hill
2020 © Ken Farfsing

ISBN: 978-0-578-46308-7

The cover art is from an oil painting by Mr. Ollie Covel. Mr. Covel was the City's longtime oil-field inspector and loved painting historical scenes from the Hill. This painting was on display in the city manager's office in city hall. Mr. Covel also painted a historical mural of the Hilltop that can be found in the city hall entry. Former Assistant City Manager Jerry Caton remembers that Ollie loved the oil field so much he would be hands-on with the oil operators, even after being warned not to by the city manager. One morning as Mr. Caton was coming to work, Ollie was in a hole dug by a contractor, covered in oil spouting from a leaking oil pipeline, at the intersection of Cherry Avenue and Hill Street.

Production services:
Populore Publishing Company
Morgantown, West Virginia

Dedication

To the Los Angeles Region Planning History Group, whose members believe that understanding the complex planning history of the Los Angeles region can help to guide the creation of its future.

To LARPHG President, Marsha Rood, and former Vice President, Steve Preston, for their leadership, vision, and assistance.

To all of the concerned planners, city managers, and urban historians, who are dedicated to preserving municipal, county, and private sector planning documents from the Los Angeles region.

Contents

Foreword

*"Municipal institutions constitute the strength of free nations. . . .
A nation may establish a system of free government, but without
municipal institutions, it cannot have the spirit of liberty. . . .
Yet, without power and independence, a town may contain
good subjects, but it can have no active citizens."*

Alexis de Tocqueville, Democracy in America, *1835*

In his tour of America, the young French nobleman Alexis de
Tocqueville was struck by the independent spirit that had sprung
up, so far removed from the European legacy of monarchy, and
he was inspired to write the early definitive account of American
democracy. His assessment of municipal government was informed
by his observation of an 1834 New England town hall meeting. The
complexities of modern life have forced all but the tiniest of communities to move beyond the direct-governance town hall model,
but a well-run town or city still demands the involvement of a free
and active citizenry. I suspect that de Tocqueville would stand by his
observations if he could observe the workings of a properly adminis-
tered modern American city, such as Signal Hill, California.

The city manager form of local government is inspired by the
genius of the Founding Fathers, who divided the functions of government into separate branches, and established mechanisms for
them to work together. For a city, a local council or board sets policy and enacts laws, and a professional manager and staff carry out

the laws. The system has proven resilient and adaptable, and with the right leadership has navigated thousands of towns and cities through unique challenges.

In Signal Hill, the unique challenges are all about oil. The quest for the black gold brought social upheaval, environmental destruction, physical danger, and a degraded quality of life. But de Tocqueville's active citizens, exercising their power and independence through their elected leaders and professional administrators, stood up, demanded better, and made it happen.

Ken Farfsing, the author of *Black Gold in Paradise,* played a key role in this remarkable story. Early in his career, Ken dedicated his administrative and organizational skills to helping people through local government. After earning his master's degree in urban planning from University of Southern California in 1980, he joined the professional staff of the City of La Verne, California, in 1981 and set about learning to apply his abilities to the task at hand. His first city manager position came in South Pasadena, from 1991 to 1996, where he learned much about the rough-and-tumble of politics in the city's struggle to prevent a freeway from dividing the small community.

He left South Pasadena in 1996, and spent the next nineteen years as city manager of Signal Hill, a community just over two square miles and then 8,500 souls in the middle of the bustling Los Angeles Basin. As manager, Ken faced any number of issues every day, from shifting federal regulations to fluctuations in the global oil economy to potholes in the streets. Over it all loomed the challenge of creating and maintaining a modern community where people and industry could both make a home.

Besides all the knowledge needed to organize a city's administration, Ken's natural curiosity led him to find out about the entire history of his home—the native American hunters, the land-rich Mexican rancheros, the cowboys, farmers and orchardists, small-town folk, and fortune-seekers who transformed the Hill time after time. When he retired from Signal Hill in 2015, Ken found that he had too many good stories to just walk away from them. The eventual result is this book. It's evident in these pages that Ken loves the city and enjoys telling about it, so *Black Gold in Paradise* is not a scholarly history. There's a wealth of factual information here, but it is not meant to be exhaustive.

There's one aside I can't resist sharing here myself. The City of Signal Hill is an enclave, a little city completely surrounded by Long Beach, with its half-million inhabitants. Signal Hill was created by the oil companies, as a way to dodge the Long Beach taxes. As the City developed its own personality, the citizens came to view Long Beach as a (more or less) friendly rival at the bottom off the hill. When Signal Hill was considering a slogan to put on its municipal vehicles, letterhead, and such, my own favorite "proposal" was "Signal Hill: We look down on Long Beach." (Predictably, our leaders rejected this.)

I believe the primary importance of the Signal Hill story lies in the interplay of resource extraction and community building. The resource here is petroleum, of course, and on a scale that would be hard to imagine for someone who has not seen it. Over a billion barrels of crude oil have been pumped out of the ground under Signal Hill, and it's still being pumped at a million barrels a year. Along with the massive industry came massive destruction and degradation of the land, and the middle chapters of this book are a sobering reminder of the cost of unregulated greed. But the people who had planted their lives and their families here demanded better, and in a decades-long process they learned how to make it happen. The particulars of the Signal Hill experience are unique, but the need to find a human balance between opposing interests is universal.

A second lesson from Signal Hill is the need for affordable housing near the places of employment, a need especially pressing in California. During Ken Farfsing's tenure as city manager, the City's population swelled from 8,500 to 11,500, with no possibility of annexing more area. Through careful, forward-looking planning, this explosive growth has been accompanied by a marked improvement in comfort and livability, and a special eye to ensuring affordable, accessible housing. The State of California has designated Signal Hill as a model community for housing compliance, and anyone who could see the comfortable neighborhoods designed for families of all income levels would agree. In addition, many of these pleasant neighborhoods have spectacular views, from downtown Los Angeles to Long Beach to Santa Catalina Island.

Maybe the most significant aspect of this story is the power—and the expense and difficulty—of redevelopment. The opportunity to fund redevelopment initiatives was given to communities by the legislature, but the road to making it happen was tortuous. A City study documented over 2,196 abandoned wells in the Long Beach Field in 2014,[1] with hundreds of abandoned wells in Signal Hill alone, and it can cost up to one million dollars per well to make the land usable. The lot where Costco now sits was owned by 2,400 individuals who had bought pieces of land in the 1920s, and each of these claims had to be resolved before the site could be developed. Not every city faces obstacles like these, obviously, but every redevelopment initiative must face the reality that money is only the beginning of what is needed.

My father had a long career as a city manager, and when I came to Signal Hill as city attorney in 1978, he warned me that the City had a bad reputation. To have been part of turning that reputation around has been the highlight of my career. The task has involved council members, mayors, business people, community activists, and ordinary citizens who care about the place where they live, and it has been a privilege to work with them. It has been a special privilege to work with Ken Farfsing through his many years as city manager, building and strengthening the municipal institutions that Alexis de Tocqueville so astutely recognized as the basis of democracy in America.

—David Aleshire
Signal Hill City Attorney, 1978 to present

Introduction

As a child, I got to know the smell of petroleum when our parents would drive our 1968 Ford Galaxy station wagon full of kids through Signal Hill, California, on our way to the Pike amusement park in downtown Long Beach. There was something exotic about the sights, sounds, and smells of the oil field. How was I to know then that someday I would spend nineteen years as Signal Hill's city manager, playing my small part in the history of a tiny city that helped change the destiny of the region, the state, and the world.

I must admit that this is a heady statement—that Signal Hill, covering only 2.2 square miles and completely enclosed by Long Beach, has had such an outsized influence. But it is difficult to overstate the importance of petroleum on the past one hundred years, and to a large extent, Signal Hill is petroleum. In the 1920s as the car craze really shifted into high gear, Signal Hill and the surrounding area produced twenty percent of the world's petroleum. The rapid development of the oil fields coincided with the equally rapid urbanization of Southern California, and created unique planning challenges that remain with us today.

Oil still influences the region, despite current awareness about how fossil fuel use damages our environment. Tremendous unlocked petroleum resources remain below Southern California. There are thirty mapped oil fields in the region, and there are still over 30,000 active wells in Los Angeles County. The petroleum in each oil field has specific characteristics, much like the human thumbprint. Signal Hill's petroleum fractures into high-end fuels

I

like jet fuels, and lower-end diesel fuel and asphalts. Other fields today produce petroleum more specific to gasoline.

Valuable lessons can be learned from Signal Hill's history, including how oil production, with proper regulation and environmental precautions, can coexist with homes, parks and open spaces, offices, stores, and industrial facilities—and also how a lack of planning and precaution can lead to almost unimaginably bleak living conditions. The story about the potential for intentional, well-managed redevelopment is equally powerful. In an era when urban redevelopment was criticized, misunderstood, and eventually defunded by the State of California, Signal Hill's forty-year effort demonstrated how this powerful tool positively altered the course of a community faced with major environmental and financial hurdles. Unfortunately, limited resources were unequal to the task of reversing every vestige of neglect and damage, but the story of Signal Hill proves that success, as a process and not a product, is achievable.

My journey to write this book really began after an April 2015 colloquium on "Black Gold in Paradise: The Influence of Oil and Energy Extraction on LA's Urban Form," organized by the Los Angeles Region Planning History Group.[1] As the city manager who had seen much of the history as it happened, I presented the basic facts on the history of the urban development in Signal Hill, and the work of the community's redevelopment agency to correct the excesses of the oil industry and to reclaim the community. Preparing for this presentation piqued my curiosity, and after the colloquium I continued additional research, coming to even a greater appreciation for the individuals and events that shaped Signal Hill and beyond.

I believe that the value of history is to help us understand how we reached this point, and to show us how to apply the lessons of the past to the challenges of the future. But as important as the bare facts are, it's also necessary to look at history through its effects on the people who lived it. This book traces several key figures in Signal Hill's history, including Jessie Nelson, the pioneering female mayor; Sam Mosher, the founder of Signal Oil; and more recent figures like Saul Price, the founder of Price Club, the forerunner of Costco. In places, this book adds a particularly human dimension to the story by turning to the memories of long-time Signal Hill resident Jonathan Booth. Booth was about eighty years old when he was interviewed in 1991 as part of the City's oral history project. He had childhood memories of the time when Signal Hill was still a sleepy farming community, and of the day when oil spewed into the air and transformed his world forever.

When my life's journey returned me to Signal Hill in July 1996 as city manager, little did I know how this 2.2-square-mile community would capture my imagination, much like when I peered out the windows of the family station wagon. My time in Signal Hill has led me on a quest to understand how this one spot of Earth has both shaped and mirrored the modern history of the world. Heady stuff indeed.

I

Native Americans, Californios, and Yankees

*"Travelers who have driven over the Alamitos and to the top
of Signal Hill never forget the wonderful panorama of sea and islands
and rolling plain and swelling hills and horizon of snow peaks.
On a clear day (of which there are at least 300 in the year)
one can see at least 20 towns and cities."*

William Galer, journalist, 1897

The romantic image of local indigenous villagers using "the hill" for smoke-signal fires to communicate with their relatives on Catalina Island is one of the City's urban legends. The image is so appealing that a Native American woman was incorporated into the City's fourth City Seal, which was created by graphic artist and then City Council Member Sarah Hanlon in 1994 for the City. There are also sentimental images of the missionaries and early ranchers using Signal Hill to watch for merchant ships, which would stop to trade or barter for animal hides and tallow. However, the name of Signal Hill is more appropriately traced back to US government surveyors in 1853. The region was sparsely settled in the 1850s, and the government survey crew established their baseline points in present-day downtown Los Angeles, Rancho Palos Verdes, and Signal Hill with large stone monuments. The first official reference to "Signal Hill" occurs in the 1889 US Coastal Survey Map based on this survey expedition.

The original stone monument placed atop Signal Hill was uncovered in 1905 by engineer E. P. Dewey, who was platting the Hilltop—as the top of the hill later came to be called—into residential lots. During his survey work he was approached by John Rockwell who was a member of the original government survey crew that set the stone monument (eight inches square on top and eighteen inches deep with a hole in the center of it) on the summit of the hill. Dewey and Rockwell located the monument, which was, fifty-two years later, now buried in two inches of soil. Mr. Rockwell recalled finding the stone in the Arroyo Seco and hauling it to Signal Hill with an ox team, a two-day trip in 1853. The present whereabouts of the stone monument is unknown.

Geologists tell us that the hill itself was formed by the seismic forces resulting from the Newport–Inglewood Fault. The fault travels on both the west and east flanks of the hill. Over the eons the bisected fault formed a pincer movement and pushed the hill to an elevation of 392 feet above sea level in what is termed an "anticline." Geologists theorize that earthquake faults act like huge underground dams, where oil deposits can collect and build up. However, there was no historic evidence of oil seeps or oil pits at the surface of Signal Hill, as existed at the nearby Rancho La Brea.[1]

The Largest Cattle Ranch in the United States

Signal Hill's history and development prior to the 1921 discovery of oil reflected the historical and development trends that influenced Southern California during the same time period. There was the period prior to the Spanish explorers, when the Tongva tribe of Native Americans lived in villages near the hill. Archeologists have documented the existence of the Povuu'nga Indian Village near Los Alamitos Ranch House and the Tibahanga Indian Village near Los Cerritos Ranch House. Signal Hill is located on the former dividing line of these two great ranchos.

Rancho Los Cerritos and Rancho Los Alamitos trace their roots back to a land grant Spanish Governor Pedro Fages gave to Don Manuel Nieto in 1784 for a large rancho covering over 300,000 acres of land in present-day Los Angeles and Orange Counties known as

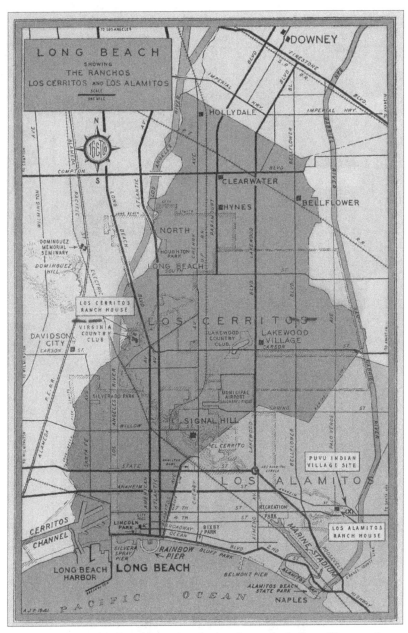

1941 map of Signal Hill and Long Beach, showing early Indian villages and ranchos. (Courtesy of City of Signal Hill.)

Rancho Los Cerritos, c. 1920s. (Courtesy of Historical Society of Long Beach.)

Rancho Los Alamitos, c. 1890s. (Courtesy of Historical Society of Long Beach.)

Rancho Los Nietos. When Manuel Nieto died in 1804 his widow and children inherited the huge rancho. In 1834, then Mexican Governor José Figueroa divided the estate's land into six ranchos. Don Juan Nieto inherited Rancho Los Alamitos (Ranch of the Little Cotton-woods) and his sister, Manuela Nieto de Cota, inherited the Rancho Los Cerritos (Ranch of the Little Hills). The present-day Alamitos Avenue was the dividing line between the ranchos.

Much of the American West and Southwest, including present-day California, became part of the United States in 1848, as a result of

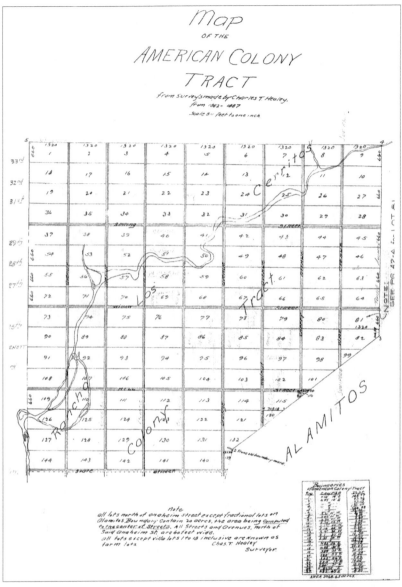

Map of the American Colony Tract, from survey made by Chas T. Healey from 1882 to 1887. Signal Hill is located at the bottom right corner of the map near the intersection of State Street and Orange Avenue. State Street is the current Pacific Coast Highway, and Vine Street changed to Junipero Avenue. These agricultural parcels established the street grid and lot patterns for future developments. The diagonal line divided the American Colony Tract from the Alamitos Tract, cutting through the present-day Hilltop, just east of the present-day Hilltop Park. (Courtesy of City of Signal Hill.)

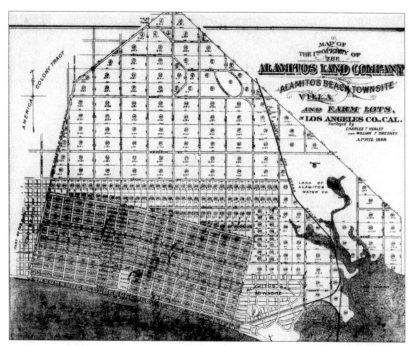

Alamitos Land Company Map of Long Beach and Signal Hill, based on an 1888 land survey, further divided Signal Hill into 20-acre parcels, which would then be further subdivided into town lots and farm lots. In the case of the Hilltop, 50-foot-wide streets were plotted running north–south on the Hill, with 60-by-130-foot residential lots. This map pre-dates the Pacific Electric Red Car route, which was approved in 1901. The US Census listed 2,252 people living in Long Beach at that time. (Courtesy of City of Signal Hill.)

the Mexican–American War. But even before the official annexation, Yankee money and ambition were beginning to exert themselves. Neither Don Juan's nor Doña Manuela's heirs managed to retain their ranchos. John Temple purchased Rancho Los Cerritos in 1843, and Abel Stearns purchased Rancho Los Alamitos in 1844.

Flint, Bixby & Co., comprised of brothers Thomas and Benjamin Flint and their cousin Llewellyn Bixby, had been raising sheep in Northern California since 1854. In 1866, they bought Rancho Los Cerritos from Temple and appointed Llewellyn's brother Jotham to oversee this southern ranch. Jotham would soon buy into the endeavor and form his own company, living on and managing the land until 1881. With the decline of the sheep industry in Southern California, Jotham sold 4,000 acres of Rancho Los Cerritos to the Englishman

William E. Willmore, who began to lay out the present-day City of Long Beach along the coast. However, Willmore went bankrupt by 1884, moving for a while to the County Poor Farm in Downey, and then to Arizona. The City of Long Beach incorporated three years later in 1887.

Stearns lost Rancho Los Alamitos at a tax sale in the 1860s due to the impacts of the Great Drought of 1862–1865 on his cattle business, once the largest cattle ranch in the United States. Without water, thousands of cattle were slaughtered for only their horns and hides. This land would transfer between a number of different owners and managers until Llewellyn and Jotham Bixby, along with their younger cousin John William Bixby, partnered with Isaias W. Hellman to purchase Rancho Los Alamitos in the early 1880s. John Bixby died suddenly in 1888 in the middle of his attempts to develop the town Alamitos Beach on rancho land. After his death, his heirs maintained control of the central section of the land, while the northern section went to the Bixby cousins and southern section went to Hellman. With this divided ownership and financial difficulties, Alamitos Beach was never realized, but would later be incorporated into Long Beach.

A land survey completed for the Bixbys in 1882–1887, known as the American Colony Tract, subdivided the Rancho Los Cerritos portions of Signal Hill into 660- by 1320-foot agricultural parcels. In 1888, the Alamitos Land Company then subdivided the Rancho Los Alamitos portions of Signal Hill into 20-acre parcels, known as the Alamitos Beach Townsite Villa and Farm Lots subdivision. These early land surveys laid out rectangular parcels, which did not address the challenges presented by the hilly terrain in both present-day Signal Hill and Long Beach.[2]

The Most Notable Cucumber Garden in the Country

Jonathan Booth recollects hearing that sometime in 1910, the year of his birth (in Oregon), his father, Charles, bought a new Flanders automobile and drove up to the low hills north of Long Beach. Jonathan remembered that his father was searching for the best location for his avocado orchard and future home. Charles's first purchases were some thirty lots located in the "saddle" between

Signal Hill and Reservoir Hill, where he would build a temporary home. Recalling his childhood years, Jonathan reflected on the quiet of the countryside, the song birds and the clanging of cow bells in the distance and the clucking of chickens. The residents living in the southeastern section of Signal Hill were primarily property owners, with some renters. Most grew their own vegetables, and raised chickens for eggs. According to Jonathan, at least one family in the neighborhood had goats. The vegetables were basic—corn, carrots, beans, tomatoes and the ever-present cucumber. The real produce growers on Signal Hill, Jonathan stated, were the Japanese.

The United States is a nation of immigrants, but attitudes towards immigrants have varied between welcoming and discouraging immigration over the years. The Naturalization Act of 1790 permitted only free white persons of "good character," who had been living in the country for two years, to apply for citizenship. In the early 1800s millions of Irish and German immigrants arrived in the United States. By 1849, the country's first anti-immigrant party—the Know-Nothing Party—was formed, as a counter reaction to the Irish and German immigrants. The Chinese Exclusion Act of 1882 is recognized as the first act in American history to place broad restrictions on a particular immigrant group.

At the dawn of the twentieth century, California had the country's largest Japanese immigrant population, which was seen by the white population as a threat to jobs. In February 1907, Japan and

Signal Hill in the background, as seen from T. L. Vore's berry farm, 1906. (Courtesy of City of Signal Hill and Signal Hill Historical Society.)

the United States entered into what is know as the "Gentleman's Agreement," limiting Japanese immigration. In 1913 the state legislature passed the Alien Land Act, which prevented "those not eligible for naturalization" from owning land for more than three years. In 1922, the US Supreme Court found that Japanese were not eligible for citizenship (Ozawa v. United States).

Prohibited from owning land, Japanese families banded together and leased large plots of land, where they grew acres of cucumbers, other vegetables, and melons. In the era prior to supermarkets, grocery stories and markets in Southern California contained fruit and vegetable sections which were exclusively operated by Japanese farmers. The *Los Angeles Times* reported that, "Japanese gardeners supplied the early eastern markets with Signal Hill cucumbers. The hill was one of the most notable cucumber gardens in the county." The 1896 edition of the *Land of Sunshine*, a publication on the farming business, reported there was an association of lemon growers in Signal Hill with twelve members. W. H. Reider grew lemons on the southern and eastern slopes of the hill. Reider reported that he kept his trees for about ten years and gradually sold off his holdings. Another lemon grower, Gerald Wall, recalled that he and his father used mules to uproot their trees and they went out of the lemon business. In 1921 these former lemon groves would be producing oil; however, another kind of development would first sweep over Signal Hill.[3]

Lemons and blossoms in a Southern California grove, c. 1910. Agriculture dominated the region at the turn of the century—lemons, cucumbers, beans, and melons were common in Signal Hill before being uprooted to make room for derricks. (Wikimedia Commons, public domain.)

II

The Road to Suburbia

"Water made imperial Los Angeles possible; but it was real-estate
development and a phantasmagoria of attendant activities—
buying, subdividing, building, selling, and finance ... within the
decade of the 1920s ... An oil boom fueled this emergent economy,
together with a tourist industry energized by Hollywood....
Between 1920 and 1930 two million Americans migrated to
California. Three-quarters of these, or 1.5 million, settled in
Southern California. Of these, some 1.2 million settled in
Los Angeles County alone."

Kevin Starr, Material Dreams:
Southern California Through the 1920s

In 1892, Anton Anze and Joe Denni were operating the Denni-Reeves Cheese Factory in Signal Hill. Moving from successful cheese makers to real estate developers in 1904, they would inadvertently be at the forefront of Signal Hill's transformation from an agricultural community to a growing residential community to one of the world's most prolific oil fields. Perhaps they discussed a vision for another Beverly Hills, located in southeast Los Angeles County. No doubt, they dreamed of real estate wealth. Most certainly, however, they did not comprehend that by the early 1920s, their small-lot, residential subdivisions would become the location of some of the densest oil well drilling in the nation. They could not have imagined that in 1925 the oil from Signal Hill would double the ship traffic in the Panama Canal. They most certainly did not comprehend that a massive

A rendering of Long Beach, 1887. (Courtesy of Signal Hill Historical Society.)

clean-up effort, beginning in the 1970s, would be necessary to rebuild the community after oil production had abated.[1]

The Region's First Master Plan: Ride the Big Red Cars

Residential real estate speculation in Signal Hill was very much influenced by the Pacific Electric Red Interurban line to Long Beach from downtown Los Angeles, which began service in 1901. Since its founding as Willmore City in 1883 by William Erwin Willmore, Long Beach had been struggling to attract attention and had poor rail connections to local and eastern markets. Local wags tied the lack of growth to deed restrictions allowing only three saloons in the entire town. Willmore died penniless on January 1, 1901. He was described as an "idealistic planner and not a practical businessman" by the local newspaper. Only 2,252 residents called Long Beach home in the 1900 census. However, by 1910 the population grew by 610% to 17,809 persons, the fastest growing city in the United States. By 1920, Long Beach had grown to 55,593 persons and most of them came because of the Red Car.[2]

At the turn of the century, Signal Hill was unincorporated territory in Los Angeles County, with the City of Long Beach reaching to State Street (present-day Pacific Coast Highway). In 1901, the City of Long Beach received an unsolicited franchise agreement to operate a high-speed electric interurban line, from Los Angeles, from

A Long Beach–bound train leaves the central 6th and Main Street Station, 1951. For decades, this was the hub that connected Los Angeles to the ever-increasing number of surrounding suburbs. (Courtesy of Pacific Electric Railway Historical Society.)

Pacific Electric interurban cars 1240 and 1222 in Long Beach, 1938. (Courtesy of Pacific Electric Railway Historical Society.)

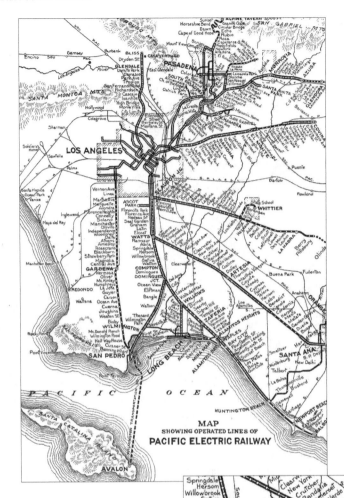

MAP
SHOWING OPERATED LINES OF
PACIFIC ELECTRIC RAILWAY

Map showing the lines of the Pacific Electric Railway, connecting downtown Los Angeles to new sprawling developments, c. 1930s. The first P. E. line approved was the route from downtown Los Angeles to Long Beach, which started operating on July 4, 1902. Signal Hill was not yet a city, but there was a generous number of rail stops serving the Hill—at least five stops: Burnett, Searby, Signal Hill, Temple and Zaferia. The Zaferia station was a junction at the intersection of Redondo Avenue and Pacific Coast Highway where the trains could continue to Newport Beach or south on Redondo Avenue to Long Beach. (Courtesy of Pacific Electric Railway Historical Society.)

William Hellman and Henry Huntington. No doubt, Huntington was a man with a vision, noting that, "It would never do for an electric line to wait until the demand for it came. It must anticipate the growth of communities and be there when the home builders arrive—or they very likely are not to arrive at all, but go to some other section already provided with arteries of traffic."

Huntington retained Epes Randolph, the engineer for the Southern Pacific, to design the master plan for the new rail system. Randolph's master plan linked downtown Los Angeles with the growing region. His master plan anticipated the region's major population centers, including Long Beach. Developers and land speculators at the turn of twentieth century might not have seen Randolph's hand at work, but the lines facilitated suburban development and foreshadowed the planning for the region's freeway network a half century later.

Spencer Crump documented the construction of the Long Beach line in his classic book *Ride the Big Red Cars, How Trolleys Helped Build Southern California*. He likened the coming of the Red Car to Long Beach and Signal Hill as an awakening ("was to awaken") . . . "The task of obtaining the property was fairly easy for it had been

1906 ad from the Los Angeles Times *promoting beach resorts made accessible by the Pacific Electric Railway. (Courtesy of Pacific Electric Railway Historical Society.)*

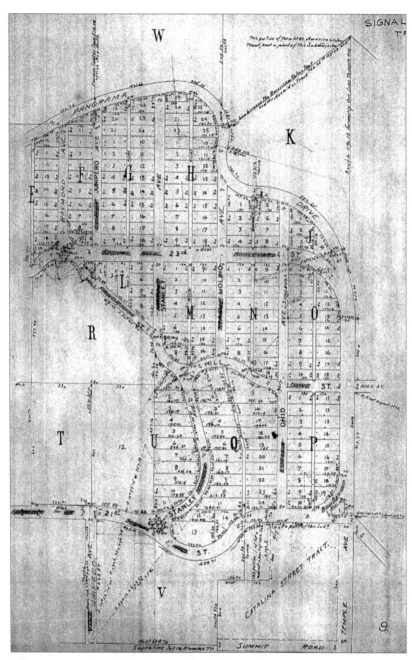

1905 tract map created by the Signal Hill Improvement Company. (Courtesy of City of Signal Hill.)

established that railroads brought great increases in land values. Property owners, most of whom purchased the land for $5 to $15 an acre, envisioned their immediate areas blossoming into cities." The Pacific Electric right-of-way would become the southern boundary of Signal Hill when the City incorporated in 1924.

Crump described the first trial car run from Los Angeles on July 3, 1902, and the crowds who arrived in Long Beach to celebrate Independence Day: "By the afternoon a crowd of 30,000 men, women and children were swarming over the little village. Most of the visitors came via the new trolley line, but a substantial number of people from nearby farming areas were attracted to view the novelty of the electric interurban cars." The city was deluged, with the Pacific Electric running cars every fifteen minutes, beginning at six in the morning.

Sanborn Map Company's fire insurance maps for the area demonstrate how urban development clustered along the light rail line. The Red Car station in Signal Hill stretched from the present-day Cherry Avenue to Walnut Avenue. At first the station serviced residents, and farmers running boxcars of produce to downtown Los Angeles. In later years the station would be expanded to handle oil loading, including a tank farm. The Pacific Electric would run special trains with tank cars loaded with crude and refined product. With the construction of the Jessie Nelson Academy in 2008, the Long Beach Unified School District would discover evidence of the prior oil uses at the long-gone Red Car station when they graded for the new school. That project would require major soil cleanup under state supervision.[3]

"The Most Beautiful Home Site in Southern California"

The Red Car drove early real estate speculation. "Dirt is Flying on Signal Hill Electric Line" ran an advertisement for the Crescent Heights Tract, which was recorded in 1904. Lots were priced at $400 to $600 per acre. G. W. Hughes was the developer. The Signal Hill Heights subdivision was recorded between Willow Street and California Avenue, and lots went on sale on June 6, 1905. The *Long Beach Evening Tribune* ran an advertisement that "Twelve Fine Villa Lots" were delightfully situated with ocean and hill views, one block from the Burnett Station of the San Pedro, Los Angeles & Salt Lake Rail Road. Artesian water was piped to every lot. The lots were 100 feet by 130 feet in size and priced at $450 to $600. It is doubtful, even at that time, that there was a view of the ocean; however, that would change with the next major subdivision in 1905.

Hughes took on a partner for continued land development activities; he and former cheese maker Joe Denni formed the Signal Hill Improvement Company. Their subdivisions differed from the early land surveys, in that they attempted to lay out the streets and residential lots to take advantage of the hill's topography and views. Their improvement company financed the gravel and oil for the streets, and planted trees and shrubs to beautify every lot. Innovative for the time, all of the electrical and telephone wires were placed underground. Water mains and electricity were laid to service every lot in the tract. The tract contained its own electric and water plant. The Hilltop tract maps plotted residential lots at 60 feet in width by 130 feet in length. The tract map illustrates serpentine streets, like Panorama Drive and Canton Drive, attempting to adapt to the steep hillside terrain.

The tract map recorded in 1905 by the Signal Hill Improvement Company recorded 228 small lots on the Hilltop. Only time would tell that a good number of the lots and streets were unbuildable due to the terrain. The new subdivisions' power plant was located in one of Signal Hill's canyons and was turned on Friday, November 3, 1905. A large 2,000-candlepower spotlight was erected atop of the Denni elevated water tower. The *Long Beach Evening Tribune* reported that hundreds of Long Beach citizens turned out to view the new light, as if there were a "new planet discovered." However, unlike a planet that moves on the horizon, this light "shone on and on at the same point." The article went on to describe the gasoline-powered, 30 horsepower electrical generator.

Taking a cue from chamber-of-commerce advertising of the day, a 1910 Signal Hill Improvement Company real estate brochure called Signal Hill the "Most Beautiful Home Site in Southern California," noting, "Like the central gem of a diamond tiara, sits Signal Hill in

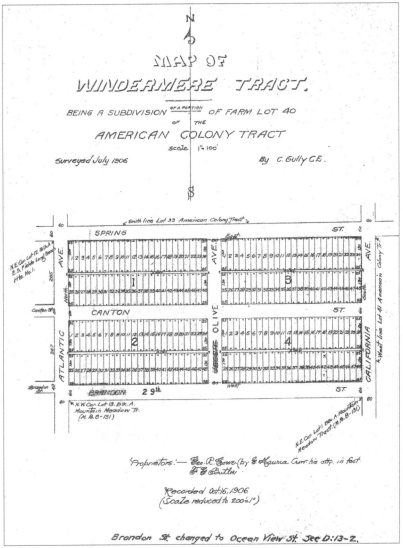

1906 Map of the Windermere Tract, a subdivision of the American Colony Tract, by C. Gully. The area of rolling hills was located southwest of the intersection of Atlantic Avenue and Spring Street. The tract was originally intended for the construction of small houses. These small lot subdivisions sprouted up in numerous Southern California communities adjacent to the Pacific Electric Railway lines. There is no evidence that any homes were ever constructed. This area would become one of the most drilled in areas in the Signal Hill Field, as the Newport–Inglewood earthquake fault crossed the property, allowing oil to pool against the fault line. At the depths of the Great Depression, in 1933 the area would be the site of the spectacular explosion and fire from the Richfield Absorption. (Courtesy of City of Signal Hill.)

the midst of this incomparable valley ... The improvement of this natural mountain park, and the creation of one of the most beautiful and attractive residence locations in the entire world, has been in progress for the past two years. During that period the Signal Hill Improvement Company, following an elaborate and artistic plan, has constructed five miles of splendid boulevards and driveways, laid nine miles of permanent concrete walks, installed a perfect water and electric light plant, thus literally transforming the hill into a thing of beauty and joy forever...."[4]

A view of the Palla mansion. (Courtesy of City of Signal Hill.)

G. W. Hughes now had other, greater ambitions for the Hilltop. In December 1910, he gathered a group of property owners to discuss building a pavilion and large telescope on Signal Hill to attract tourists. (Neither was built.) At the meeting, $2,800 in stock was sold in the Trackless Trolley, Inc., to operate a bus line up the Hill. The buses were to have 20-horsepower engines and

A monumental Denni family headstone, Sunnyside Cemetery, Long Beach.

seat twenty-four passengers. However, area excitement really grew as the Los Angeles Federated Improvement Association announced their support for the Southern Branch of the University of California to be located in Signal Hill. The Association's Garner Curren stated that "Los Angeles will not get the University as it will not be desirable to place it in the city, but it should be situated between the city and the sea, and close to both."[5] Mark Keppel, county superintendent of schools at the time, attended the meeting and supported the $5 million State budget amount, but there were several alternative locations discussed. The school was eventually located in Westwood and is known as the University of California, Los Angeles (UCLA).

From 1905 until the discovery of oil in 1921, a series of grand residences were constructed on the Hilltop. These included Joe Denni's mansion, which covered half a block of the Hilltop area, with its own water tower and distinctive decorative block walls and electric outdoor lights. The Palla mansion was constructed adjacent to the Denni mansion, taking up one-quarter of the block. Andrew Palla intended his mansion for a group retirement home. All of the homes took advantage of the spectacular views towards Long Beach, Catalina Island, and the Pacific Ocean. More modest homes

To the best of Jonathan Booth's memory, there were no paved streets in Signal Hill in 1918. This southwest view from Panorama Drive up Junipero Avenue shows the street grading and the Hilltop water tank from the Signal Hill Improvement Company. (Courtesy of City of Signal Hill.)

were being constructed near the Pacific Electric Red Car line. Some of the decorative block walls from the Denni mansion still existed into the late twentieth century, and paying homage to the area's residential past, their design was incorporated into Hilltop Park, Discovery Well Park, and the surrounding residential subdivisions constructed in the 2000s.[6]

A Terrestrial Paradise of Eternal Sunshine

The Signal Hill Improvement Company described Signal Hill's weather in their real estate sales brochure as the "American Italy." The promotional pamphlet went on to claim "there never was a fairer spot, and Signal Hill is the central star of this land of sunshine." Civic boosters for Southern California uniformly advertised the region for its mild weather and sunny days. Residents moving to Signal Hill in the early 1900s did not know that the region was subject to the influences of the ocean temperature pattern named El Niño and to recurrent epic flooding from what meteorologists now call "atmospheric rivers."

In fact, the region experienced massive flooding in 1832, 1859, 1862 and 1868. The rains in 1862 were particularly intense, with thirty days of uninterrupted rainstorms, dropping over fifty inches of rain on downtown Los Angeles during the season. The flatter portions of Signal Hill, with its ranches and farms, were at risk of inundation. As the region gained more residents and businesses in the 1880s, additional costly floods, in 1884 and 1886, started the discussion of how best to control the floodwaters.

It was less than a decade after residential lot sales began on the Hill, that the floods of February 1914 left no doubt that the region would need to control flooding in order to save lives and property. It had started raining in November 1913, and the ground was saturated when three days of storms began on February 18, 1914. Although downtown Los Angeles received only seven inches in the storm, portions of the San Gabriel Mountains received upwards of ninety inches of rain. Every major stream and river in the region overflowed.

The Los Angeles River discharge was measured at 31,400 cubic feet per second, equal to the flow of the Colorado River. Long Beach and Signal Hill became an island. The Lakewood area became a vast lake, flooding hundreds of homes and ranches. All railroads, highways, and telephone lines into Los Angeles were swept away. It was estimated that four million tons of silt and debris were washed into the Long Beach and Los Angeles Harbors, in some places stranding ships in eighteen feet of silt. The flooding had a disastrous impact on the harbors, which by 1914 had become a major economic engine for the region, with the federal government constructing the breakwater and major railroads now serving the area.

After the 1914 flood, Los Angeles County began planning dams and levees; however, local land owners were unwilling to pay for the improvements as made clear in the defeat of bond issues in 1926 and 1934. It was not until the massive regional flooding on New Year's Day of 1934 that the federal government decided to step in and manage and fund the necessary flood-control improvements. After—as in 1914—three days of continuous rain, a wall of mud, water, and rocks tore through La Cañada Valley, killing forty-nine people. Twelve people were killed at an American Legion hall, which was being used by the Red Cross as a shelter, when rocks tore through the building's walls. Forty-five people were never found. A break in

Prior to the installation of the Hamilton Bowl and California Bowl, flooding periodically inundated the lower portions of Signal Hill. Pictured are people wading through floodwaters on Pacific Coast Highway, c. 1920s. (Courtesy of City of Signal Hill.)

This photo shows the Hamilton Bowl—now called Chittick Field—in the 1930s. The area first collected petroleum but was converted to a flood control basin by the Los Angeles County Flood Control District after severe flooding in the 1930s. (Courtesy of City of Signal Hill.)

the Los Angeles River levee north of Long Beach again inundated the Lakewood and Signal Hill area.

The county board of supervisors requested $19.3 million from the Great Depression–era Emergency Relief Appropriation Act funds to construct sixty-four separate projects, ultimately costing $99.9 million. One of the projects constructed was the Hamilton Bowl (later known as Chittick Field), which had at one time been used to hold oil from Signal Hill's wells. The Hamilton Bowl became one of a series of detention basins constructed throughout the region, including the California Bowl, which was constructed south of Spring Street and east of California Avenue.[7]

America Needs Petroleum—Lots of It!

Oil has been a part of California since prehistoric times. Spanish explorers found local natives gathering asphaltum from natural seeps and using it a number of ways, including to waterproof baskets and canoes. Andres Pico collected oil from the seeps found in Pico Canyon, near Newhall, distilled it and used it to illuminate the San Fernando mission. Interest in the oil seeps was heightened after the discovery of oil in Pennsylvania in 1859. The first well drilled in California was in 1861 and located in Humboldt County. Well drilling was largely unregulated in the nineteenth century.

The State of California Division of Oil and Gas's predecessor (the Mining Bureau) required oil well permits beginning in the 1890s, and it began tracking the oil companies operating in the state. The August 1921 *Directory of California Oil Operators* compiled by the Division (created in 1915) illustrated that over 480 oil companies operated up and down the state, in 45 oil fields stretching from San Diego to Fresno, with 14 active fields in Los Angeles County alone. The US Bureau of Mines reported in December 1921 that California produced almost 19% of the nation's oil, with its 7 million of the 39 million barrels of oil pumped annually nationwide. The Signal Hill Field had yet to become a major factor in 1921.

Of course, the arrival and impacts, including fuel needs, of the "car age" are a big part of the story. In 1900, there were an estimated 8,000 vehicles in the nation. With the unveiling of the Model T by Henry Ford in 1908, registered vehicles had grown to 458,500 by 1910. In order to deal with the onslaught of vehicles, California formed the Department of Motor Vehicles in 1915 and registered 191,000 vehicles. By 1917 there were 4.8 million vehicles on the nation's growing highway network, resulting in a nationwide gasoline shortage in 1919. In Los Angeles in 1915, there were 8.2 residents per vehicle; by 1925 there were 1.8 persons per vehicle. Car sales boomed in the 1920s, and by 1929 there were 26.7 million registered vehicles in the United States. By 1930 California had over 2 million registered vehicles.[8]

Having been a Signal Hill resident for about seven years, in 1917, Charles Booth began construction of his new bungalow-style home, which his son Jonathan recalled moving into on November 11, 1918, as the rest of the country celebrated the end to the Great War. The postwar years were special for the young boy, and he reminisced about fishing in a small stream just east of Reservoir Hill. His mother would fry up the small fish he caught. However, the best time was during the summer, when school was out. Jonathan and his friends would go quail hunting with their slingshots. In the fall, when the grass on Signal Hill had browned, Jonathan and his friends made wooden sleds to scoot down the Hill, since real snow was over one hundred miles—and many months—away.

Like most of their neighbors, the Booths had a small orchard and grew many of their own vegetables. As Jonathan recalled, reflecting back several decades, the paradise was about to end: an intruder was about to appear, and the intruder was named petroleum.

III

The Discovery of Black Gold

"There she came! There was a cheer from all hands, and the spectators went flying to avoid the oily spray blown by the wind. . . . she made a lovely noise, hissing and splashing, bouncing up and down! . . . the news affected Beach City as if an angel had appeared in a shining cloud and scattered twenty-dollar gold pieces over the street. You see, Ross-Bankside No. 1 'proved up' the whole north slope; to tens of thousands of investors, big and little, it meant that a hope was turned into glorious certainty. You couldn't keep such news quiet, it just didn't lie in the possibility of human nature not to tell . . . as soon as the pipe-line was completed . . . its owner would be in possession of an income of something over twenty thousand dollars every twenty-four hours."

Upton Sinclair, Oil!, *1927*

Geologists suspected that oil lay beneath hills north of Long Beach. The first well drilled in the area was in 1917, by the Union Oil Company. Known as Bixby No. 1, the well was located near the intersection of Wardlow Road and Long Beach Boulevard. The well was drilled to 3,449 feet and came up dry—a "duster." History would show that the well was drilled too far north and too far west of the active field.

Geologists from Royal Dutch Shell also had a suspicion that oil was stored beneath Signal Hill. D. H. Thornburg, one of these Shell geologists, who grew up in Long Beach, remembered playing in Signal Hill in his youth and spotting marine fossils and tilted strata on the Hilltop. By 1919, Shell had begun mapping some of the more promising geological formations in Los Angeles County, with the help of Thornburg. Of course, locals and others were well aware of the oil companies' accelerating exploratory activities in the area. But, despite the excitement and potential for riches, success was anything but guaranteed.

> Charles Booth's son Jonathan recalled being present for the spudding in of the E. J. Miley well on March 5, 1921, his eleventh birthday. He thought he would be present for the start of a historic drilling operation. However, the Miley well was beset by mechanical problems, and ended up being a dry hole instead.

In April 1920, Shell leased 240 acres on the east face of the hill for an exploratory well, known as Alamitos No. 1. The "spud date" of Alamitos No. 1 was March 23, 1921, the first day that the well was drilled. Exactly three months later, workers would find traces of oil after they brought up the drill bit, and later that day, Alamitos No. 1 growled and oil shot into the air over 114 feet. At the same time, two Shell Oil Company officials were headed to Signal Hill to shut down this wildcat well. Shell had just decided they had put in enough effort into Alamitos No. 1 without results so far, and they were ready to pull the plug on their own exploratory well, thinking they lost on the gamble, much like the Miley well had turned out to be fruitless.

The *Long Beach Press* covered the historic event in their June 24th edition. The workers capped the wellhead and prepared the "Discovery Well" for pumping, which began on June 25, 1921. In its first day, the Discovery Well flowed 590 barrels. The barrel measurement dates from the original discovery of oil in 1859 in Pennsylvania. At the time the fledging petroleum industry decided that a barrel would consist of 42 fluid gallons, or 300 pounds of oil, as the standard measure. Within two days, the Discovery Well flowed 1,200 barrels per day. In no time at all, the word spread, ushering in nearly a century of oil production in Signal Hill. By 1985, the Discovery Well had produced over 700,000 barrels of oil and continues to produce to this day.[1]

Oil-Field Workers, Gamblers, Bunco Men, and Prostitutes

Every day after school, Jonathan would hike up to Alamitos No. 1 to inspect the drilling operation. On June 23, 1921, he watched as workers brought up the drill bit, dripping in mud and water. There were only four people on the derrick floor at the historic moment— two roughnecks, the driller and Jonathan. The driller peered down and saw water gleaming in iridescent pools. He dipped one of his fingers into the pools of water then licked his finger.

Jonathan probably didn't lick his fingers, but he did hear the driller reverently exclaiming, "Boys, we done got ourselves an oil well!" Jonathan raced home with the news. "Dad!" He panted, "They struck oil in the Shell well! I saw it!" Charles Booth set his newspaper aside, stopped puffing on his cigar and exclaimed, "We'll, I'll be chewed up and spit out. That should change things up here, Jonny Boy—yes, sir . . . and maybe not for the better."

The Long Beach Press *front page, June 24, 1921, the day after the first major oil spout on Signal Hill. (Courtesy of City of Signal Hill, scrapbook.)*

Signal Hill in 1922, with relatively few wells. Looking north from Pacific Coast Highway. The Pacific Electric line is visible, with the tracks in the bottom left and catenary wires above. (Courtesy of City of Signal Hill.)

By the time the Shell Company officials reached Alamitos No. 1 that day, a wave of excitement had already taken hold. Signal Hill was on its way to becoming a boom town, seemingly overnight. Hotels and rooming houses in Long Beach filled to capacity. Some residents of Signal Hill turned their homes into boarding houses. Long Beach soon reached the 100,000 population mark. Andrew Palla's mansion, originally built as a multi-resident retirement home, was purchased by Shell Oil for worker housing. It seemed as if derricks were appearing in a blink, in the middle of houses. There was no room for the steam boilers, so they were erected in the streets. The oil drilling frenzy was well underway by late 1921. Landowners insisted that drilling begin so as to not be left behind. Signal Hill's prior development of town lots facilitated extremely dense drilling. One of the consequences of over-drilling was that the field stopped producing naturally; by 1924, oil companies found it necessary to install pumps.[2]

Jonathan Booth recalled that his father, Charles, lost a million dollars while his friends got wealthy on oil royalties in the 1920s and beyond. These friends had been neighbors-to-be. In 1918, Jonathan Booth's mother, desperate for neighbors, had persuaded Charles to sell some of his Signal Hill lots near their home to their Long Beach friends. So, he sold ten of his lots to friends at his cost, under the condition that the friends build their homes on these lots. The homes were never built; the friends leased them to oil companies, once oil was discovered.

The original San Pedro, Los Angeles & Salt Lake Railroad line into Long Beach in 1925 was located on the east side of California Avenue and is now the residential neighborhood of Las Brisas. The Sunnyside Cemetery in Long Beach is in the top right corner. The bridge in the center of the photograph was constructed at Willow Avenue to cross above the rail line. (Courtesy of City of Signal Hill.)

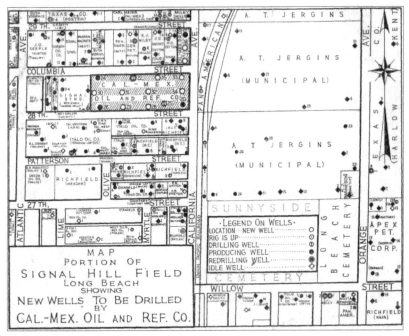

Map, c. 1920s, showing existing and new wells to be drilled in a portion of Signal Hill. (Courtesy of Signal Hill Historical Society.)

Still, with the discovery, Jonathan's father was besieged by "lease hounds" seeking oil leases. Landmen from dozens of oil companies, from large to small, from reputable to fly-by-night, camped out at the Booths' front door. Landowner Charles, who had studied mining engineering in Montana, decided to organize the neighbors and called a meeting of area landowners to review the lease offers. In April 1921, they executed a community lease with the Vernon Oil and Refining Company for what would become known as the Booth wells.

The postcards of the 1920s idealized homes located in the oil field, playing to the image created for tourists of life in Southern California. However, the reality of the impacts of the oil field on adjacent homes was far from ideal.

Signal Hill, populated with significantly more wells than just a few years before. (Courtesy of Signal Hill Historical Society.)

Ten months after the Discovery Well had been in active production, Signal Hill boasted 108 oil wells, producing 14,000 barrels per day. By 1923 there were 270 wells being drilled at one time. New production horizons were discovered at 5,000 feet below the surface, and the field began to expand from the Hill area. By 1924 the field produced 259,000 barrels of crude oil per day. This represented one-third of the entire oil produced in California, which was the nation's top producing state. The "rush to produce" had its consequences. As a later California Division of Oil and Gas

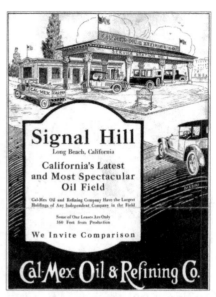

Cal-Mex Oil & Refining was one of the first companies to bring in new wells in an area one mile north and west of the Discovery Well, adjacent to the Sunnyside Cemetery, in October 1922. (Courtesy of City of Signal Hill.)

report stated, "there was no thought given to well spacing, areas of drainage, or possible damage to neighbor wells. Also, little attention was paid to well courses, resulting in many crooked holes, some of which drifted under neighboring properties." So many trespass lawsuits were filed in Signal Hill, that a state law was approved in 1935 that abrogated the lawsuits beginning March 13, 1936.[3]

Oil-field workers were in great demand, and it seemed that there were never enough workers. Wages were high—drillers were paid $10.50 per day, and roughnecks up to $9.00 per day. Newly arrived workers who could not find housing erected shacks in the middle of roads, with drivers forced to drive around them. Similar to mining towns, next came the "oil-field camp followers." These included the standard assortment of gamblers, bunco men, and prostitutes. Even with Prohibition, liquor was available from local bootleggers. A *Signal Hill Leader* 1926 article reported that the Signal Hill Police Department raided a home at Walnut and Creston and confiscated

Aerial view, from the south looking north, c. 1930s. (Courtesy of City of Signal Hill.)

The Denni mansion was soon surrounded by active oil wells. (Courtesy of City of Signal Hill.)

four cases of whiskey. The gamblers built shacks filled with pool tables, slot machines, tobacco counters, and card tables. The shacks were built with back escape doors.[4]

"You'll Never Make a Thin Dime Just Lookin' On"

Contemporary observers noted that there was a "carnival atmosphere" in Signal Hill. Large circus tents, similar to ones used by popular religious revivals at the time, were erected for potential investors. Advertising in local papers and in flyers attracted potential investors to Los Angeles's Pershing Square, where buses were chartered to Signal Hill and the promoters' tents. Investors were enticed with free meals and get-rich-quick sales pitches. Newspapers from the early 1920s carried articles that explained how oil

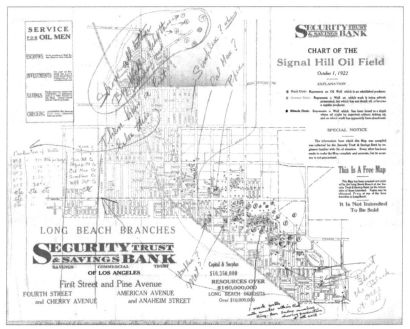

In order to assist small investors in speculating on oil wells, financial institutions often provided maps of the oil field. Chartered buses ran from downtown Los Angeles to Signal Hill for tourists and locals alike to see for themselves the hustle and bustle of the oil field. Many of the visitors fell under the spell of "oil fever" and purchased stock certificates in the new companies. The largest stock swindle of the time involved the Julian Petroleum Company, which operated wells in Signal Hill and other oil fields. (Courtesy of City of Signal Hill.)

wells would make money with "pipeline easement" deeds. One article stated that "receipts from the sale of oil are free from all costs and paid in direct cash by the pipeline company . . . This is [the] working man's well, rich men and capitalists can never control this project."[5]

Upton Sinclair's 1927 historical novel *Oil!* includes an apt description: "Scattered here and there over the hill were derricks, and the drilling crews were racing to be the first to tap the precious treasure. By day you saw the white puffs from the steam engines, and by night you saw lights gleaming on the derricks, and day and night you heard the sound of heavy machinery turning. . . . The newspapers reported the results, and a hundred thousand spectators read the reports, and got into their cars and rode out to the field where the syndicates had their tents, or through the board-rooms in town, where prices were chalked up on blackboards, and 'units' were sold to people who could not know an oil-derrick from a 'chute of chutes.' "[6]

In California, the "rule of capture" was the law, so the person who drilled the well first and reached oil was likely to get the largest share of the pooled oil. Lease rates climbed overnight. While Shell Oil had paid Alamitos Land Company a royalty rate of one-sixth, the royalty rates would climb overnight to one-third and even fifty percent. Companies also seemed to form overnight. It was described as "oil fever," as promoters brought in visitors to hear from so-called "experts." All of the commotion in Signal Hill—the sight of the derricks, the noises and smells of oil exploration and production—was like a hypnotic trance to the crowds.[7]

Successful boosterism meant increased positioning and fighting for leasing opportunities, followed by quick mobilization and construction, as described by Walter Tompkins: "Blasé Californians, to whom oil plays were becoming somewhat commonplace by 1921, found the Signal Hill boom difficult to believe. Never had they seen such a frenzy of town-lot drilling, such irrational leasing feuds, such cut-throat royalty wars and unprecedented speculating. The scramble for Signal Hill drill sites became so competitive that in many places the legs of tall wooden derricks interlaced each other. . . . Speculators swarmed in like vultures."[8]

An aerial photograph looking southeast towards Signal Hill, c. 1930s. (Courtesy of Historical Society of Long Beach.)

Celebrated circus owner, showman, and businessman P. T. Barnum was famously supposed to have said, "There's a sucker born every minute." Signal Hill's most infamous promoter was Chauncey C. "CC" Julian. His most famous quote was "You'll never make a thin dime just lookin' on." The Julian Petroleum Company ("Julian Pete") first appeared in the Huntington Beach Oil Field in 1921. Julian was successful in drilling a well that at first produced 1,200 barrels per day. The well's production dropped after eight days to 32 barrels per day. Julian was ready to move on from Huntington Beach to Santa Fe Springs, another "land of opportunity," thanks to oil fields.

The consummate bunco man, his Julian Petroleum Company had 40,000 stockholders and $11 million dollars within its first month of promotion, and moved into Signal Hill in 1923. In an era when news was beginning to spread nationwide through the radio, Julian Petroleum Company was known throughout the nation. It appeared that, overnight, the former oil worker had made it rich; he dressed in tailored suits and was driving a Pierce Arrow. Julian's success was not just in conning tourists and farmers to buy oil stocks, but as one banker was quoted, "The more intelligent people are taking a shot at it."

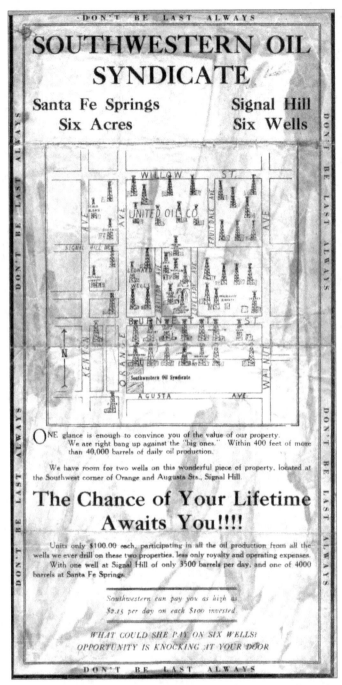

A newspaper ad by the Southwestern Oil Syndicate telling the reader "Don't be last always." (Courtesy of City of Signal Hill, scrapbook.)

Nevertheless, in 1927, Julian was forced to sell the company after losing feuds with bankers and stockholders. Wells were drilled that had come up dry or did not produce as expected. Julian left for China where he committed suicide, never to return to Signal Hill. However, the fraud had not yet run its course. The new owners of Julian Petroleum Company, S. C. Lewis and Jack Bennett expanded on Julian's deception. Borrowing $800,000 from local bankers, they formed stock pools. They persuaded Motley Flint, of Pacific Southwest Trust and Savings Bank, to invest heavily in the company. This imparted the air of respectability to the company.

Investors were enticed into investment pools by what appeared to be large profits, at first. The first pool returned $790,000 on $1 million in initial investment. Six hundred thousand shares of stock had been authorized for sale, and almost three million shares had been sold. On April 25, 1926, the pool failed and the stock prices plunged, despite pronouncements by Flint that "everything is absolutely okay." Lewis and Bennett were indicted and a scandal erupted when they were acquitted, with accusations that District Attorney Asa Keys had taken bribes. Lewis and Bennett went on to another swindle and eventually served jail time. Motley Flint was murdered by an upset investor. The swindle resulted in the loss of $150 million.[9]

In 2007, the City of Signal Hill came the closest it has come to physically identifying the presence of Julian Petroleum Company in the City. At that time, the City's redevelopment agency began a major land acquisition project, eventually purchasing four blocks of vacant land at the southeast corner of Spring Street and Atlantic Avenue. Title research revealed that Julian Petroleum Company had recorded easements on the four lots on the corner and had recorded a pipeline easement that ran parallel to Spring Street. Ironically, there are two abandoned wells in the vicinity. It is unknown if these were drilled by Julian Petroleum, but with nearly one hundred years of hindsight and with technology not available to drillers in 1920s, it's now clear that these wells, drilled west of the Newport–Inglewood Fault, missed the most productive zones in the field.

The United States was on track to produce over 900,000,000 barrels of oil in 1927. That year, as the Roaring Twenties were coming to an

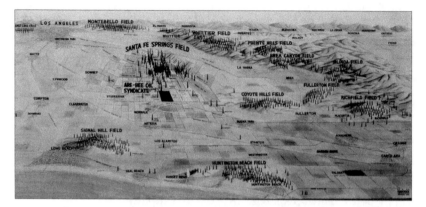

Signal Hill was not the only place in Southern California with oil. This 1922 map shows active drilling sites throughout the region. See page 203 for an enlarged version and 204–205 for additional views. (US Library of Congress, public domain.)

end, the *Saturday Evening Post* carried a story about overproduction of oil in the nation. Town-lot drilling was cited as one of the causes, and the article highlighted the Signal Hill Field, with photographs, as an example. By 1929, a Conservation Committee was established by the California Oil Producers, in an attempt to curb overproduction. Cities and towns impacted by the rapid exploitation of oil needed to start reining in oil and bringing order to chaos—both for market and economic reasons, and because current practices were taking a devastating and unsustainable toll on these communities.[10]

Widespread Ruin: "A Glistening Lake of Oil"

Oil exploration and development was at first poorly regulated. This resulted in damages to Signal Hill's existing residences and farms, as nascent residential neighborhoods and agricultural uses were rapidly overrun. Fires from the field's natural gas were very common in the early years. Shell's second well was a "gasser" (a gas pocket was hit), which immediately blew out and caught on fire. It was estimated that the well flowed at twenty million cubic feet of gas per day, until the fire was extinguished three days later. It took a combination of seventeen steam boilers pumping water to bring the fire under control. A third well, Shell's Martin No. 1, required one hundred pounds of dynamite to extinguish its fire. The fire engulfed eleven other derricks and three gassers.[11]

These fires and oil well blowouts caused much damage to the surrounding fields and homes. As one *Long Beach Telegram* article described, "Machinery, trees, telegraph poles, and buildings are torn to bits and scattered with a sea of mud over large portions of the landscape." It told of one blowout that covered a house two hundred feet

Men building dikes to contain oil after the Richfield refinery fire, June 2, 1933. (Courtesy of City of Signal Hill.)

Postcard highlighting the prosperous civic development in Long Beach and the industrial development of Signal Hill in the background. From afar, the environmental effects of the oil field aren't apparent, c. 1930s.

A Signal Hill well blowout, coating everything in its path in a layer of oil. (Courtesy of City of Signal Hill.)

A house and trees badly damaged after a nearby well erupted. (Courtesy of City of Signal Hill.)

away with "mud, oil, and rocks . . . ruined the trees in the yard, bespattered and half wrecked the family automobile, and left the lawn covered with an eight-inch coat of oil, mud, and rocks." Air quality was also a problem, with raw gas spewing into the area. Furthermore, fog captured the gas, and sparks could set off explosions.

The largest blowout in Signal Hill's history occurred on January 23, 1922, when the Black & Drake well erupted. The *Long Beach Telegram* reported that a six-block area of the Hill was covered with a "rain of oil and sand." The newspaper article went on to detail a scene of desolation—the well was a mess of wrecked timbers and the surroundings were a "glistening lake of oil." Willow Street contained four inches of oil and mud, and cabbages and lettuce protruded from a nearby vegetable farm appeared to float on top of the oil. The ruin to homes and lands on Signal Hill was widespread. The home of J. A. Benson was soaked in oil, pouring through cracks in the closed windows and doors, drenching furnishings, and his palm trees dripped with oil.[12]

Oil-field work was hard and hazardous, with serious injuries and death occurring routinely. Oil wells could be drilled without pressure control valves. Workers were injured and killed with gas and oil blowouts or with resulting explosions and fires. The local newspapers reported stories about the death and injuries to oil-field workers. The October 2, 1925, edition of the *Signal Hill Beacon* carried the gruesome details of the death of David Patton, who was accidentally killed in an oil accident. His body was discovered by his nephew who went to look for him after midnight at the Patton and Cassidy well. Patton's body was entangled in the machinery, which had stopped the well from pumping.[13]

Sam Mosher Sees an Opportunity

Before the petroleum craze of the 1920s, fortune-seekers had been planting citrus trees, not oil rigs, in Southern California. In 1842, a frontier trapper named William Wolfskill was looking for a place to invest his earnings. As a naturalized citizen of Mexico, he was eligible to purchase land, so he bought a ranch near Los Angeles and began growing grapes, oranges, and lemons. With the US annexation of the region after the Mexican War, the discovery of gold in 1849, and California statehood in 1850, Wolfskill's agricultural enterprises made him a wealthy man, and made citrus growing a tempting beacon to entrepreneurs.[14]

A vast citrus empire grew in Southern California, stretching from Santa Paula to Riverside and from Upland to Orange County, through the San Fernando and San Gabriel Valleys. Land agents marketed the area, especially to Eastern investors, as "frost free," which was not entirely true. Freezes were rare, but only five hours of temperatures below 26 degrees would destroy an entire season's crop, and a week of cold could kill the trees completely. Replanting was costly, and it could take up to seven years for a tree to be productive.

One of those infrequent freezes hit Whittier in 1922, and one of the farmers who lost his lemon crop was Sam Mosher. Mosher had been born in Carthage, New York, and when he developed poliomyelitis at an early age, his family moved to California under doctors' recommendations. Mosher earned a degree in agriculture from UC Berkeley in 1916, and no doubt planting a citrus grove seemed like a natural next step. But after the 1922 freeze, which wiped out his crop, he decided he had had enough of trying to build his future on the fragile trees. Discouraged, he read about the excitement in Signal Hill, and one day drove down to see what all the fuss was about.

Mosher recalled that from seven miles away, the Hill seemed to be in a virtual fog, from the steam boilers powering the rigs. At five miles away the noise from the drilling sounded like "remote thunder," and that, "The ear-numbing cacophony of an oil field, especially in the era before electricity and diesel power replaced steam for drilling and pumping, could be bewildering to the uninitiated." Well casings, sucker rods, and drill pipe clanged on delivery trucks. Traveling blocks clashed against the derricks and pipes. The venting of gas from wells roared.

Mosher also noted half-finished rigs, slush pits, and pipe racks. There were "fire hoses and steam lines to climb over, supply dumps, makeshift roads, vaulting over open pipeline trenches waiting to be backfilled, and dodging traffic." Where pipelines existed, they were an "inconceivable snarl of pipes, conduits, sewage, cables and sewers for the transmission of oil, natural gas, sewage, and electricity, steam, water, telephone and telegraph wires." There were no permits required and no inspections for any of this work. Trench diggers worked at night, to avoid the expansion and contraction problems with their iron pipe from the heat of the day. Leaks were common and difficult to locate. Where pipelines did not exist, Mosher recalled seeing gasoline traveling downhill in ditches along Orizaba Avenue. Derrick fires and explosions of tanks and refineries were a common occurrence.

To Sam Mosher, all of this looked like opportunity. He borrowed $4,000 from his mother and founded Signal Hill Gasoline Company. One of his first moves was to invest in a simple device to condense wet gas from the wellhead—extracting what is known as casing head gasoline. He self-built the petroleum condenser from free plans he obtained from the US Interior Department. From this

Right, Sam Mosher, c. 1920s. who founded the Signal Oil and Gas Company in 1922. In his later years, he was a regent of the University of California, and he owned a 4,500-acre ranch (Dos Pueblos) west of Santa Barbara, where he grew citrus and raised millions of orchids annually. He died in 1970 at seventy-seven years of age. (Courtesy of City of Signal Hill.)

Gasoline transfer station, circa 1920s. (Courtesy of City of Signal Hill.)

A Signal Oil truck refuels a plane at the Los Angeles Municipal Airfield, 1931. (Courtesy of University of Southern California, on behalf of the USC Libraries Special Collections.)

initial investment, Mosher built Signal Gasoline Company into Signal Companies, one of the largest conglomerates in the nation. Besides interests in oil production, refining, and a network of gasoline stations, later Signal Companies went on to own a 48% stake in the American President Lines, a Pacific ship line. Signal Companies also owned Mack Trucks and the Laura Scudder innovative food company, and held a stake in Golden West Broadcasters, which had radio and television interests in the California Angels and the Los Angeles Rams. Mosher became a partner in the American Independent Oil Company, which was involved in oil production in the Middle East.

Mosher's early success far outpaced that of other petroleum entrepreneurs largely because he recognized the value of marketing and knew how to grow a business. His Signal Gasoline Company—also operating under the name Vernon Gasoline and later Signal Gas and Oil Company serviced a network of local gasoline stations from their refinery. The company eventually grew to include an extensive network of filling stations throughout the West.

Signal Gas was known for its "Purr Pull" advertising campaign, which boasted that the gas "will make a motor purr on the hard pull." Additionally, the gasoline was colored with a purple vegetable

New Signal truck at a Signal Oil and Gas Company LA Bulk Plant, 1932. (Courtesy of University of Southern California, on behalf of the USC Libraries Special Collections.)

Signal Purr Pull gas station and auto laundry ("car wash"), 1931. (Courtesy of University of Southern California, on behalf of the USC Libraries Special Collections.)

dye, which made it stand out in the clear glass cylinders atop the gas pumps. Signal's effective advertising also included promotional items aimed at children, with the expectation that families would frequent Signal gas stations for the toys. Other marketing strategies aimed at children included the "Carefree Carnival" radio program in 1930, and sponsorship of the popular "Tarzan Clubs" during the Great Depression.

Starting during the war, in 1942, Signal sponsored "The Whistler," a weekly radio mystery drama aired by CBS in its Western region and in Chicago. Each episode opened with the sound of footsteps and a haunting whistled tune, followed by the host's announcement: "That whistle is your signal for

Gas pump, with the claim that this gasoline "Stops 98% of Knocks," 1932. (Courtesy of University of Southern California, on behalf of the USC Libraries Special Collections.)

Tarzan, Jane, and ape, 1932. Photo taken to promote the Signal Gas and Oil–sponsored radio show. (Courtesy of University of Southern California, on behalf of the USC Libraries Special Collections.)

Tarzan Club, Lake Los Angeles, 1933. (Courtesy of University of Southern California, on behalf of the USC Libraries Special Collections.)

the Signal Oil program, The Whistler." A total of 692 episodes were produced, until the program ended in 1955.[15]

Signal Hill in Print

In the thirties, Southern California became the focus of the suddenly huge military aircraft industry, and Signal Hill joined the effort with even more petroleum production and refining. Over sixty percent of the total aerospace manufacturing for the war effort occurred in Southern California, and it changed the character of the entire area. Ansel Adams, the famous nature photographer and environmentalist, documented the bustle for *Fortune* magazine in 1939. Adams visited Long Beach, where Douglas Aircraft was manufacturing the B-17 "Flying Fortress" bomber and reconfiguring its DC-3 into the C-47 "Skytrain" military transport. Adams took a side trip to photograph the famous Signal Hill oil field, where he was especially struck by the derricks standing on seemingly every piece of ground. *Fortune* published some of these Adams photographs in its February 1940 issue.

The Palla mansion on the Hilltop was purchased by Shell Oil to serve as a dormitory for oil-field workers. (Ansel Adams, Ansel Adams Fortune *Magazine Collection, Los Angeles Photographers Collection / Los Angeles Public Library.)*

Sunnyside Cemetery, Long Beach, 1939. Ansel Adams donated his collection of two hundred photos of Southern California to the Los Angeles Public Library. The Library decided to reimburse Adams $150 for the entire collection. (Ansel Adams, Ansel Adams Fortune *Magazine Collection, Los Angeles Photographers Collection / Los Angeles Public Library.)*

Cemetery Statue and Oil Wells, Long Beach, California, *by Ansel Adams, 1939. By far, one of Ansel Adams's most captivating photos related to the ramp up in defense manufacturing in Southern California was this angel in the oil field. In the background is a portion of the Signal Hill field with its numerous derricks. The derricks are long gone, replaced with pumping units. However, the angel remains in Sunnyside Cemetery to this day watching over Elizabeth Colvert, who died in 1914. (Collection Center for Creative Photography, University of Arizona. © The Ansel Adams Publishing Rights Trust.)*

IV

A City Is Born: Incorporation and Early Struggles

"We want a good, modern town when the derricks are gone.
We contemplate building a city hall, a fire department,
a library, schools, and maybe a jail."

—*Don C. Bowker, Signal Hill's first city attorney, June 6, 1924*

The 1920s were a pivotal time in Southern California. The oil boom, with its attendant upheavals, swallowed everything that had come before it. "Millions of dollars of new income poured into Los Angeles, undermining the social structure of the community, warping and twisting its institutions, and ending in debacle (the stock market crash) ... For Southern California the decade was one long drunken orgy, one protracted debauch."[1]

From June 25, 1921, the first day of production for the Discovery Well (Alamitos No. 1), oil production and oil-related uses took precedence and dominated Signal Hill's early economy. Oil exploration and production created environmental and planning legacy issues, including soil contamination and improperly abandoned oil wells and pipelines. These legacy issues would require that future generations make substantial and continuing investments to return the

57

land to safe and productive uses, including consolidating unbuild-able lots sold to multiple buyers by oil speculators.[2]

Concurrent with Southern California's growth, the City of Long Beach was attempting to develop their harbor. In the era prior to state constitutional property tax limitations, cities could impose added property taxes for public improvements without a vote of the people. The City of Long Beach moved to annex Signal Hill. The Signal Hill oil companies grew concerned that their taxes would more than double if they were incorporated into Long Beach, so they promoted and financed the anti-annexation effort. However, forming a new city required local citizen support.

How Long Must Women Wait for Liberty?

The City of Long Beach, the oil companies, and the residents in Signal Hill could not have realized in 1924 that the effort to incorporate Signal Hill would hinge upon two historic women. One of these women, Susan B. Anthony, would become a national figure as founder of the women's suffrage movement in 1878. The other, lesser known, would become the first mayor of Signal Hill—Jessie Nelson. The 19th Amendment to the US Constitution would give women the right to vote in 1920, a mere four years prior to Signal Hill's incorporation.

Congress first took up the issue of the women's right to vote in 1878, with the Anthony Amendment. The issue was polarizing, and Congress would not confront the women's right to vote for another forty years. Anthony—the abolitionist, educational reformer, labor activist, temperance worker, and suffragist—worked tirelessly for the women's right to vote. Anthony was arraigned in 1872 for voting in the City of Rochester election. At her trial in 1873, the judge ordered the jury to have no discussions, and she was found guilty. She was fined $100, which she refused to pay. By 1877 she had gathered petitions from twenty-six states, with over 10,000 signatures, to submit to Congress. She testified at every session of Congress from 1877 until her death in 1906 for the women's right to vote. She would not live to see the passage of the 19th Amendment, but other women carried on the fight.

On June 17, 1917, six women faced a judge in Washington, DC, for holding up banners in front of the White House urging President Woodrow Wilson to support the women's right to vote. These suffragists would become the first of many to face charges of obstructing traffic with their protest. Found guilty and given the choice to pay a twenty-five dollar fine or go to jail for three days, the women chose jail time. Women's suffrage was not on President Wilson's agenda, since he depended upon conservative Democrats from the Southern states as part of his power base. However, Wilson had just been re-elected in November 1916 and decided to meet with the suffragists. At the meeting, he refused to endorse their agenda and angrily dismissed the delegation. The next day twelve women took up banners demanding "MR. PRESIDENT, HOW LONG MUST WOMEN WAIT FOR LIBERTY?"

A protest movement was born, and the White House was the scene of protests for another five months. The protests became a tourist attraction to some and hated by others. Protesting women were branded as unpatriotic. In late June, counter protestors ripped down the banners and more women were arrested and jailed. Sixteen of the women were given sixty-day jail sentences. More violence ensued, and the government's reaction angered and motivated more women to travel to the nation's capital. Mary Nolan—at seventy-three the oldest of the jailed suffragists—struggled with the male guards. Lucy Burns, who had taken the leadership position after Anthony's death, was handcuffed to the prison bars. The prisoners resorted to a hunger strike and were force-fed.

Lawyers working for the jailed women were finally successful in getting them their day in court. The court hearing was a media circus. The judge called the testimony on the jail conditions "blood curdling." Newspapers described the women as haggard, pale, and disoriented, and that many had visible bruises. Three days after the hearing, the government dismissed the charges. Public opinion was turning. On January 10, 1918, the House of Representatives passed the Anthony Amendment—exactly forty years to the day after it was first introduced. The Anthony Amendment moved to the states for ratification and went into effect on August 26, 1920. Meanwhile, back in Signal Hill, Jessie Nelson registered to vote. And now, as a registered voter, she could run for office.[3]

Jessie Nelson and the Fight for Incorporation

At the time of incorporation, in 1924, Jessie Nelson had lived in Signal Hill for twenty years. She was born in 1871 and raised in Clarksville, Tennessee, and migrated to California in 1903, as a young woman, with her husband, Zechariah T. Nelson. Like many men of his time, "ZT" was interested in real estate development and bought seventeen acres of land on the Hill, the present location of the Civic Center and Signal Hill Park. He also owned property in Long Beach, known as the Nelson Business Block, at First Street. However, ZT was interested in preserving Signal Hill as a residential area free from industry. When ZT died on July 4, 1922, there were already more derricks than homes in the community.

Jessie Nelson took an interest in local affairs, even though the area was unincorporated county territory. She was an active member of the Signal Hill Civic Improvement League. In an ironic twist of fate, in 1911, Jessie Nelson and the League petitioned the City of Long Beach to place a monument to William Willmore at the pauper's section of Long Beach Municipal Cemetery, since Willmore had been buried there in an unmarked grave. The cemetery was located adjacent to Signal Hill. In comments before the Long Beach City Council, Jessie Nelson asked, "do [you] not think it incumbent upon the City of Long Beach to erect a fitting monument, not only as a matter of sentiment, to perpetuate the memory of the founder of this city, but as a matter of history, that the grave may not be lost to the public?"

Voter registration records from 1926 list Jessie Nelson as "housewife." However, this description does not fit the complex and complicated person found in historical records. As a local reporter, she contributed columns on Signal

Signal Hill's first mayor, Jessie Nelson, with her husband, c. 1920s. (Courtesy of City of Signal Hill.)

Hill and Long Beach to the *Long Beach Press* and *Long Beach Daily Telegram*. One of her newspaper articles in the *Telegram* (November 17, 1921) covered the fire at Shell's Martin No. 1, and the great damage that it caused to adjacent residences and properties. During the Great War she was active with the Red Cross and in bond drives. She became active in establishing a county library in Signal Hill, and she later worked in forming the Signal Hill Library. She was intent upon Signal Hill receiving its due: "This was another case of taxation without representation. We paid $20,000 to the county for a library tax, but we had no library. We paid the county road tax of 35 cents, per $100 valuation, making a $140,000 road fund. We paid $500,000 to Long Beach for schools, but we had no schools."[4]

As the movement to annex Signal Hill to Long Beach gathered steam, Jessie Nelson became active in her opposition. Her major concern was that the property owners and residents of Signal Hill could not afford to pay the higher property taxes. It was largely through her activities that the annexation movement was defeated. She became interested in Signal Hill becoming its own city. The local paper reported that Jessie Nelson and Petroleum Midway Company worked for the incorporation. The records also show that Jessie Nelson had leased her property for drilling rights to the company.

The incorporation election was held April 7, 1924, at the home of Jessie Nelson, with 344 "yes" and 211 "no" votes. Signal Hill was incorporated on April 14, 1924, when the Los Angeles County board of supervisors canvassed the election results. The population upon incorporation was 1,806. Jessie Nelson was elected as the president of

City seal, 1924. This is the original corporate seal, which included a depiction of oil wells, the Palla mansion, and the Denni Hilltop water tower—the major landmarks of the time. It's unclear if the fourth symbol is the image of a tree, or perhaps it's an oil gusher? (Courtesy of City of Signal Hill.)

the City's first board of trustees (later to be called the city council). It was a small city, less than two square miles in size, surrounded by the City of Long Beach on all four sides. The city limits included much of the then-known oil field and was bounded on the south by the Pacific Electric Railway right-of-way. The city incorporators also set the city limits ninety feet back from the existing streets along Atlantic Avenue and Wardlow Road.[5]

A Monumental Choice

As a condition of cityhood, new cities are required to negotiate a property tax revenue transfer with their host county. In what would prove to be a fateful decision, Signal Hill agreed to incorporate as a "low property tax" city. This designation did not mean that the property tax levy would be relatively less in Signal Hill than other cities; the tax levy remained essentially the same after incorporation. The term actually relates to how the tax revenue collected is divvied up.

All counties and cities in California receive property taxes, and many special districts and school districts receive property taxes as well. Prior to the incorporation of a city, the county would levy and collect all the property taxes and share them with the local school districts and other special districts. When a city incorporated, it negotiated for a share of the county's property taxes, under the assumption that the city would be replacing county services— such as sheriff and fire—with their own city departments, and they needed a revenue source to fund these municipal services. Then, as now, property taxes were the single largest source of discretionary revenues for many counties and cities.

Prior to the 1950s, the County of Los Angeles negotiated a large share of the property taxes to newly forming cities to fund municipal services. It was common for cities like Los Angeles, which incorporated in 1850, and Long Beach, which incorporated in 1897, to receive over twenty-five percent of the total property tax revenues collected by the County in the territory of the new city. This revenue sharing "generosity" by the County came to a halt in 1954, with the incorporation of the City of Lakewood. In what became known as the "Lakewood Plan," cities would contract with the County for services and

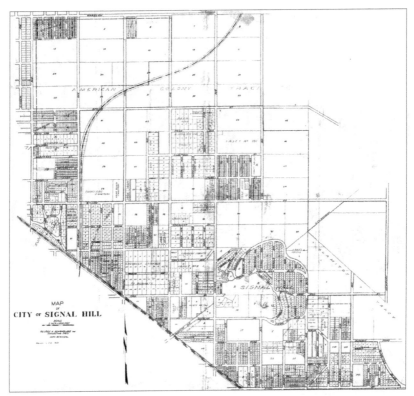

Map of Signal Hill, 1925. The City's engineer prepared this composite map of the land subdivisions just after the incorporation of the City. The City's southern boundary was the Pacific Electric Red Car line and State Street (Pacific Coast Highway). There were still large lots north of Willow Street, but much of the oil field was overlaid by the residential subdivisions approved by Los Angeles County prior to the City's incorporation in 1924. (Courtesy of City of Signal Hill.)

be limited to 7%, or sometimes even less, of a share of the property taxes. Over forty-three cities would incorporate as low property tax cities in Los Angeles County following the Lakewood Plan.

Signal Hill was the forty-first city to incorporate in Los Angeles County, during the time period when the County was more generous to the cities with their property tax revenue allocations. However, since Signal Hill was forecast to be one of the wealthiest cities in the region based on oil revenues, the negotiated agreement required that the City forgo a large share of the property taxes. In 1924, there was certainly an abundance of revenues to support the City of Signal Hill for the foreseeable future. However, this fateful decision would

Between 1913 and 1923, eleven acres of Signal Hill were owned by silent film studio Balboa Amusement Producing Company—based in Long Beach—and used for outdoor shoots. Buster Keaton and Roscoe "Fatty" Arbuckle were two prominent Balboa stars who had films shot in Signal Hill. Above, a group of actors and their bicycles take part in shooting a movie at the corner of Pacific Coast Highway and Redondo Avenue, c. 1920s. (Courtesy of Historical Society of Long Beach.)

Signal Hill was also the home to the Southern California Military Academy, shown here in the 1920s. The private, all male academy operated from 1924 to 1987, serving students from kindergarten through 9th grade. The school was located at 1900 21st Street near Cherry Avenue. The Academy property was purchased and demolished by the Long Beach Unified School District for the construction of Alvarado Elementary School, which opened in 1990. (Unknown photographer, Security Pacific National Bank Collection / Los Angeles Public Library.)

come back to challenge the City in future decades, as oil field revenues began to decline along with declines in oil field production.[6]

"The Wealthiest City, Per Foot, in the US"

Prior to incorporation many families were forced to leave Signal Hill. Their properties did not contain oil; however, the adjacent oil operations rendered their properties worthless. Properties could not be sold or even rented. Jessie began to work on bringing these families back to the Hill. She petitioned Southern California Edison to lower electric rates to residents. When it was reported that a widow was unable to care for her three children, Jessie Nelson requested that the City establish $15 in a bank account for food for the family.

She began to exert her considerable influence to bring a new elementary school to the growing community. City council minutes from September 15, 1924, show that the new mayor was interested in working with the Long Beach Unified School District and began meeting with school officials. Then, in February 25, 1925, she reported to the board of trustees that her negotiations were successful and that the new school was being advertised for construction bids. Jessie Nelson would not live to see the new school open. Fighting an undisclosed illness, she resigned from the board on April 2, 1925. She

Among Nelson's top priorities was seeing to it that a school was brought to her new city. Signal Hill's first elementary school, pictured here, was later destroyed in the 1933 Long Beach earthquake. (Courtesy of City of Signal Hill.)

had attended all thirty-eight board meetings from her swearing in less than one year before, on April 11, 1924.

Jessie Nelson passed away on August 24, 1929, at the age of fifty-eight. The *Long Beach Press Telegram* reported that she died at her home on Cherry Avenue. The news accounts at the time indicated that the first year of hard work after incorporation had broken her health. The *Press Telegram* reported that her chief accomplishments had been related to improving the condition of Signal Hill residents whose properties had been ruined by the flow of oil.

Local newspaper articles at the time indicated that Jessie Nelson was the first female mayor in California. Research, however, shows that women were mayors of the cities of Sunnyvale, Carmel-by-the-Sea, and Susanville predating 1924. However, these women were not the *first* mayors of their communities. Jessie Nelson was in a class by herself as the only woman mayor at the helm of a newly incorporated city. And, it wasn't just *any city*, but a city with an assessed value of $42,036,135 at the time of incorporation. This was a very sizable sum in 1924.

The *Los Angeles Times* calculated that "this huge, taxable valuation, compared to its trifling size, made Signal Hill the wealthiest city, per foot, in the US. Having only 1,500 population, the town's per capita wealth, based on the assessed valuation, was $23,332." It would be another twenty-three years before another woman was elected to the city council. Interestingly, the City purchased seven acres from the Nelson estate in 1932 to construct the new Civic Center and Signal Hill Park. Plans for the city hall were approved in January 1934. In a fitting tribute to her dedication to education and the community, in 2012 the Long Beach Unified School District honored the City's request to name Signal Hill's first middle school the Jessie Nelson Academy.[7]

Creating a City Overnight

The first meeting of the board of trustees, in 1924, was held at the Civic League Clubhouse (Lemon Avenue and 23rd Street) and adjourned to the basement of the Hinshaw residence on Cherry Avenue. In order to support municipal services, the City levied a tax

The first city hall of Signal Hill, c. 1925. (Courtesy of City of Signal Hill.)

of $100 for every well and tank in the community, raising $94,000 in 1924. In the second fiscal year, the board of trustees levied 42 cents on every $100 dollars of valuation, with 10 cents for the fire department and 4 cents for the library. Until the tax funds were secured, General Petroleum provided credit to Farmers & Merchants Bank to back up the city warrants.[8]

At the first trustees meeting, demands were made to the County for funding, and permits were issued to the City of Long Beach to construct water and gas lines to serve Signal Hill. At this meeting, oil companies also applied for agreements to construct oil pipelines in the streets. By the second meeting, on May 12th, the board accepted a petition to annex more territory to the City, bounded by State Street (Pacific Coast Highway) and Redondo Avenue. From July to September the City moved five small buildings into Signal Hill to serve as the temporary city hall.

The early meeting agendas were dominated by the need to bring order to chaos. There were so many unpaved roads in the new town that by September 1925 a recall election was underway of two board members, over street-paving projects. Working under the California Street Improvement Act of 1911, the trustees began assessing property owners for road improvements. The initiative, sponsored by the Voters and Taxpayers Protective Association, would have required that city voters approve of paving projects. The trustees also adopted an ordinance prohibiting the moving of houses into Signal Hill without permission from the City.[9]

The new city council needed to provide for police and fire services, as the community transitioned away from the county sheriff and county fire department. The board held two emergency meetings when the city marshal, the chief law enforcement official, abruptly resigned. One of the marshal's responsibilities was to deal with dogs running amok in the community. However, the council continued to organize the community's public safety. Two years after incorporation, the editor of the *Signal Hill Leader,* Roy E. Shadle, commented that the city was "well policed, considering the small force. No street brawls. Bootleggers reduced to the lowest possible minimum."[10] The council meeting on August 16, 1926, was interrupted by the Signal Hill Fire Department responding to a derrick fire. The local paper reported that members of the public left the meeting to watch the parade of trucks go by.

By October 1924, the trustees were considering licensing drugstores for the sale of medicinal alcohol. In February 1925, the trustees approached the Pacific Electric Railway with the request for "feeder routes" of their buses to serve the community from the Red Car stations. The City was regulating rooming houses by June 1926, and it received a request to build and operate a wrestling arena. The trustees denied a petition from Mr. Roy Possom to operate a billiard parlor. At their June 16 meeting, all boxing, wrestling, and pool halls were unanimously forbidden in the City.

Not limited to just considering public safety and roads for the new community, the trustees called a city-wide public meeting in October 1925 to review purchasing the water system. The new city was originally served by the Long Beach Water Department. The City reported that $300,000 in bonds would be necessary to purchase and build a new water system. It would not be until 1930 that the City would purchase the water system from Long Beach, including two water production wells. Between 1931 and 1935 two additional wells were drilled, and an elevated tank was constructed on the Hilltop. The City also contracted with Long Beach for its sewer services and did not have a municipal sewer plant until 1936.[11]

The three most discussed items on the early council agendas were waste oil in streets, oil ditches obstructing driveways, and abandoned oil sumps and derricks. Even though the City's first comprehensive oil code was not adopted until 1942, the trustees were active in regulating the oil companies. Late in 1924, they adopted strict guidelines on the length and size of pipelines. Every council meeting had an item on oil companies, whether it be a citizen complaint or the granting of an oil pipeline franchise. In May 1924, it was suggested that each "leading" oil company in the city participate in discussions on how to resolve the issues of oily water and mud from wells running into ditches in city streets.

There were also several agenda items during the first year of incorporation regarding pipelines placed in city streets without permits. The trustees discussed property cleanup where oil well sumps and abandoned derricks had disfigured the community. A city committee was appointed to examine the nuisances caused by rubbish burning. Another committee examined the disposal of waste oil in the community. The trustees received a petition from residents opposed to a gas dehydration plant. The marshal was directed to

Cherry Avenue is being widened in this picture of the Hinshaw Building on the northeast corner of Cherry Avenue and 21st Street, c. 1920s. Starting in the late 1920s, the building served as the City's second city hall, until a new one was constructed in 1934. (Courtesy of City of Signal Hill.)

address the issue of oil, mud, and water running down city streets. Finally, by October 6, 1924, the city adopted an ordinance prohibiting the overflow of oil on city streets.[12]

Refineries in the 1920s were not centralized, as became the common practice in later years. Early on, generally the oil companies and the city officials cooperated. However, there was one refinery in 1924 that caused a major noise nuisance, and the trustees appointed a subcommittee to deal with the problem when a petition from 119 residents was received. The Buena Vista Refining Company, located just south of Hill Street and north of the Red Car line, attempted for several months to mitigate noise and odor problems. By September, the residents were accusing the trustees of siding with Buena Vista Refining and allowing the refinery to "seize their properties without compensation."

In October, the trustees pursued a civil case against the refinery, when residents' complaints continued. The city marshal indicated that it would be difficult to find a jury, since anyone within hearing distance from the refinery would not qualify. However, General Petroleum requested time to assist Buena Vista Refining with the noise issues. By February 1925, the noise and smell issues at the refinery had been resolved. However, the complaints about the smells and noises of refineries would continue from the residents, until Signal Hill's last refinery, operated by Chem-Oil, partially burned down and closed in 1994.[13]

The Great Depression Comes to Signal Hill

At the end of the 1920s, the United States had the largest economy in the world—yet, the economy was a "house of cards." There is no single explanation for what caused the Great Depression. The causes included overconcentration of wealth, structural weaknesses in the banking system, and that consumers had overreached during the Roaring Twenties and were in debt for cars and homes, and they had borrowed money to invest in the stock market. The stock market collapse of October 24, 1929, became known as Black Thursday for good reason. Nervous investors began selling overpriced stocks, with a record 12.9 million shares sold in one day. Black Thursday was then followed by Black Tuesday, October 29, where another 16 million shares were traded after another panic was set off on Wall Street.

At the end of the panic, many stocks were essentially worthless. Those who purchased stocks with borrowed money were completely wiped out. The market collapse began a series of chains of events resulting in a decade of worldwide economic upheaval known as the Great Depression, which ushered in dramatic social changes including the rise in fascism and the sowing of seeds for World War II.

With the collapse in the stock market, came consumers' loss of confidence in the economy. Industrial production began falling, and for those lucky enough to have jobs, wages were cut. Investors began to panic, and there were runs on banks in the fall of 1930. Investors were demanding their deposits back in cash. During the next three years over half the nation's banks closed—9,000 banks in all, which meant $2.5 billion in deposits vanished. Automobile manufacturing in the United States fell 75% from 1929 to 1932, with over half of the automobile manufacturers going out of business. In 1929 alone, auto manufacturers lost $413 million (over $3 billion today).

By 1930, there were 4 million unemployed workers, growing to 15 million unemployed by 1932, a full 20% of the entire population. The Great Depression had impacts on oil production and usage worldwide. The price per barrel of oil dropped 66% in value, from its 1926 price. The largest oil strike then known on US soil came on October 5, 1930, in Tyler, East Texas, further lowering the price of oil by 10 cents per barrel. The petroleum market was in chaos, with attendant impacts on Signal Hill.

The country was ready for change and elected Franklin D. Roosevelt as 32nd president of the United States in November 1932. During his election campaign, he had promised swift action within the first one hundred days of assuming office. Roosevelt pursued the New Deal, where Congress approved fifteen new programs designed to restore confidence in the economy. A key component of the New Deal focused on investing in public infrastructure with the creation of the Public Works Administration (PWA). One of the more successful programs was the Civil Works Administration (CWA), which was created in 1933 to put employed Americans immediately back to work. In all, the PWA financed the construction of over 221 government buildings in California from 1933 to 1939, benefiting both large and small cities.[14]

The "Therapy of Public Works"

With all the economic uncertainty, it is hard to believe that the city council moved forward with the construction of a new city hall at the depths of the Great Depression. California historian Kevin Starr aptly described the investment in infrastructure in the 1930s as the "therapy of public works."[15] The city council embarked on their first major public works project only six years after incorporation and during a period of great economic uncertainty. After having offices in temporary buildings since 1924 and holding council meetings in the basement of council member Hinshaw's house and then in the Hinshaw Building on Cherry Avenue, it was time for a new city hall regardless of the Great Depression.

By March 1930, the city purchased five parcels from the estate of Jessie Nelson for $17,000. The escrow closed in September 1932, and the council approved a contract to have Jessie Nelson's home and garage relocated in December of that year. The January 4, 1934, council minutes show that Kenneth Wing was to be the new city hall's architect. Wing is now considered a very significant architect for his contributions to Los Angeles County and Long Beach architecture. He was born in Colorado Springs, Colorado, on January 11, 1901. His family moved to Long Beach in 1918, where he attended Polytechnic High School. He received his bachelor's of science in architecture at the University of Southern California in 1925. Wing opened his own architecture firm in 1930—gambling during the Great Depression that his business would make it.

The Signal Hill City Hall was one of Wing's earliest jobs with his own company, which thrived. Wing would go on to have a career that spanned five decades. The Long Beach earthquake of 1933 significantly increased his business; he was retained to design and reinforce dozens of Long Beach schools. His new schools were designed in the WPA/PWA Moderne style, including Jordan High School, Alexander Hamilton Junior High School, and Luther Burbank Elementary School. He was also the architect for Pasadena City College.

Among Wing's early works, he is best known for designing the main terminal for Long Beach Airport, which would open just before the beginning of World War II. He would later go on to design the Carmelitos Housing Project, the Long Beach Memorial Hospital, and numerous private homes throughout Southern California. He designed the second Long Beach City Hall and Library, which opened in 1976. Both, however, were recently demolished, having been replaced by new facilities in 2019.

The city council minutes in early 1934 show a flurry of activity related to the new city hall: the council accepted Wing's plans and the structural engineering for city hall on January 2, bids were opened for lumber on January 8, bids were awarded for steel on January 10, and bids for plumbing were accepted on January 22. The council also approved the cornerstone, along with a time capsule full of memorabilia. By March, the council was reviewing photos and reports on the construction.

There are references in the minutes to sending construction reports and photographs of the construction to the Civil Works Administration in Los Angeles. Construction was completed August 6, 1934—in eight months. The first city council meeting was held in

City hall was constructed at the depths of the Great Depression in an eight-month period in 1934. Rainfall records reveal that 21.6 inches of rain fell in downtown Los Angeles that year, making it one of the rainiest years on record. City council minutes from the time reported that the US Civil Works Administration was involved in the project. These inspection photos show the riveted steel post and beam construction of the superstructure. (Courtesy of City of Signal Hill.)

Signal Hill City Hall, c. 1935. (Courtesy of City of Signal Hill.)

City hall's main floor reception area, public counter, and office areas. The vault at the left was retained and used as a separate mailroom and copy room when the city hall was seismically upgraded and renovated in the 1990s. (Courtesy of City of Signal Hill.)

the new city hall three days later, August 9, 1934. Perhaps a future historian will determine if the construction was financed by a loan from the CWA, but the CWA reference in the minutes makes sense since the CWA started its operation in 1933. In any event, city hall has served the community well for the last seventy-five years, having been significantly remodeled in the early 1990s. Hopefully, it will continue to serve the community well for a long time. It should be rightfully seen as a landmark of the vision of a city council struggling with the uncertainties of the Great Depression.[16]

V

The Depths, and a Plan to Rise Out of Them

It wouldn't be until 1962, when the City adopted its first general plan, that Signal Hill would begin to dramatically rehabilitate itself over the course of decades to come.

—Corey Washington, journalist, 2015

Reclaiming Signal Hill is complicated and far from being a quick fix. It is ongoing. The long time frame to repair the community is due in large part to the devastation caused by the extraction and production of oil. Due to oil production, Signal Hill did not construct the public infrastructure necessary for urban development. The oil field did not require paved roads, sewers, or the other utilities necessary for orderly urban development. But also, after the boom and before the grand "city on the Hill" vision, other factors came into play that affected that first plan: In 1933, the area suffered significant damage from the Long Beach earthquake. And, for years, tax revenues from oil extraction and production were increasing; then came downturns. Overproduction related to World War II triggered oil land subsidence, and secondary recovery was used to stabilize subsidence such that early reclamation efforts involved substantial reinvestment in the oil field.

Viewed through the lenses of history, the reclaiming of Signal Hill began in 1962 with the adoption of the City's first general plan. When the great wave of suburban development engulfed Southern California after World War II, it bypassed Signal Hill, where land was tied up in oil surface-use restrictions and oil production. Reacting to being left behind in the wave of prosperity, the 1962 General Plan envisioned a grand "city on the Hill." The general plan illustrated six-story residential, commercial and office buildings, with densities of eighty units per acre sprouting from the Hilltop. The plan summarized the community's feelings that it would be a "tragedy if high-quality residential, commercial and industrial uses do not replace the oil facilities now located here." This was in the days prior to the requirements of the 1972 California Environmental Quality Act.

2,900 Active Oil Wells

The Signal Hill Field is part of the larger Long Beach Field, which contained over 2,900 wells at its peak in 1928. By far the most productive part of the Field was the Signal Hill Field, which contained 1,719 wells. Drilling on fifty-foot-wide residential town lots concentrated the wells in Signal Hill and other similar areas in Southern California. One oil consultant calculated that if the oil wells had been evenly distributed, instead of concentrated, there would have been 1.2 wells per acre in the field. In some cases, oil speculators drilled 4–5 wells per acre. By the early 2010s, only 421 active oil and gas wells remained in Signal Hill, producing on average 1.2 million barrels of oil annually.

The City's oil-well consultant estimated that by 2014, over 2,196 oil wells had been abandoned in the Long Beach Field. However, the consultant also discovered that the quality of the abandonments varied; in some cases, telephone poles were simply pushed into wells and covered with dirt. Early on, these wells would leak oil and gas, creating public safety problems for the community. During the beginning of the twenty-first century, oil-well abandonments and re-abandonments were completed without any formal standards. Beginning in the 1920s, the State adopted well abandonment standards. These standards were revised over the decades in response to advances in technology and the earth sciences, and in learning the lessons from explosions and spills. Besides improperly abandoned wells, the City faced the daunting task of funding the cleanup of soil contamination and the removal of a rat's nest of abandoned pipelines.[1]

Adding an Active Earthquake Fault to the List of Challenges

In the midst of the 1920s oil boom, Jonathan Booth was attending local schools—Wilson High School and the Southern California Military Academy. His father, abandoning the aspirations he'd had of farming, invested in nearby wells himself. By 1929 the Booth family had moved to an apartment house they owned on Fifth Place, near Ocean Boulevard, because the increased drilling had finally made their Signal Hill home unlivable. The home shook twenty-four hours a day from the nearby oil drilling. There was constant noise from steam blasts, rotary drilling, pipe clanging, and the roar of truck movement. It affected Jonathan's mother so much that she demanded they make the move. The Signal Hill that Jonathan remembered from his early youth was long gone. However, the shaking from oil drilling would pale in comparison to the shaking of the Long Beach earthquake.

The same Newport–Inglewood earthquake fault that created the Hill and dammed up the oil resources, broke on Friday, March

The masonry of the East Long Beach Methodist Church was no match for the force of the earthquake. (Courtesy of City of Signal Hill.)

10, 1933, at 5:55 p.m. The Long Beach earthquake was estimated at 6.25 on the Richter Scale, which would be considered moderate by today's standards. However, many of the commercial and institutional buildings were constructed of unreinforced masonry. Especially hard-hit were the local public schools, where all of the Long Beach Unified School District schools were damaged, including the newly constructed Signal Hill Elementary School. Lucy Curtis, the school's librarian, reported that she carried armloads of books to a portion of the school that was usable. The library was eventually moved to a bungalow on campus, that was used for the kindergarten and was undamaged by the earthquake.

Nearby Long Beach Polytechnic High School was destroyed, and throughout the Southern California region seventy schools were totally destroyed. As fate would have it, the quake was in the evening, after students had been dismissed for the day, or the deaths and injuries would have been far greater. One student died as the Wilson High School gym collapsed around him. Hundreds of people were injured, and 120 people died in the quake from collapsed houses and buildings. The newspapers reported that most of the deaths occurred when people rushed outside and were hit by falling bricks and debris. As a result of the devastation, California became the first state in the nation to develop special building code for public schools. Known as

Whittier Junior High School in Long Beach, badly damaged, like every other school in the district. (Courtesy of City of Signal Hill.)

Among the buildings needed to be rebuilt was the original, brick Signal Hill Elementary School. The new school is shown here, c. 1940s, still surrounded by the active oil field. (Herman Schultheis, Herman J. Schultheis Collection, Los Angeles Photographers Collection / Los Angeles Public Library.)

the "Field Act," it was adopted in 1935, and the amended law governs school construction to this day.

Luckily, the Pacific Fleet had just returned to their Long Beach base, and the US Navy sent in emergency supplies and two thousand sailors and marines to help the devastated communities. Pictures from the time vividly show the aftermath of collapsed brick buildings, mounds of debris, smoke from fires, and broken water and gas mains. Local papers reported four major fires in the oil field. The City of Long Beach organized work crews to remove the bricks and debris from the streets, as well as to remove dangerous and leaning walls. Presumably, Signal Hill did the same.

The streets were cleared of debris in less than ten days after the quake; trucks hauled off the rubbish to the oil field areas of Signal Hill and Long Beach. The slow work of rebuilding continued for months and years afterward. An editorial cartoon in the *Press Telegram* illustrated a man hit in the head with a brick, celebrating that the Great Depression was over as he was surrounded by men hard at work rebuilding. The work of debris removal continues to this day. This debris had the unintended consequence of creating an obstacle to the development of Signal Hill; the City and developers found debris from the Long Beach earthquake when excavating for the Bixby Ridge project and for Discovery Well Park.[2]

Jonathan Booth, in his early twenties, was visiting his future wife, Maxine Rose, when the earthquake struck. A loud roaring filled the air. Jonathan, Maxine, and the Rose family poured outside of their house only to see the brick schoolhouse across the street collapse into rubble. Jonathan had come to visit Maxine by riding the bus. Mr. Rose volunteered to drive Jonathan back to his apartment house. They spotted black smoke overhead and found "Poly" High School engulfed in flames. When they arrived at the apartment house, it has been knocked off its foundation. The adjacent building had been split into two sections. The next day they visited the Booth homestead in Signal Hill. The house had survived the quake and their fourteen oil wells were pumping peacefully.

After the Boom Comes the Collapse—Literally

As the storm clouds of war gathered in May 1941, President Franklin Roosevelt declared an unlimited national emergency and created, by executive order, the Petroleum Administration for War. Appointed to head the new agency was Ralph Davies, an executive of Standard Oil Company of California. The marching orders for the new agency were to determine the increased amounts of petroleum products for the rearmament and to supply the nation's allies. In November 1941, the American Petroleum Institute met in San Francisco at their annual convention. Little did they know that by December 7th the nation would be at war with Japan and that on December 11th Germany would declare war on the United States.

In 1940, Jonathan, now nearly thirty years old, had decided to move to the Booth family homestead at the corner of 21st Street and Redondo Avenue. He had graduated from Stanford University with an engineering degree and was working for Douglas Aircraft and taking aeronautical classes at Cal Tech. World War II would change his life as it would millions of lives. Jonathan recalled that the Army set up anti-aircraft batteries on his property to protect the Hill. One night the sirens wailed, and guns started firing. Jonathan knew that he had to move his family away from the Hill.

A pool of oil (or oily water) sits on the ground below an industrial building on stilts in the Signal Hill Oil Field, c. 1937. (Herman Schultheis, Herman J. Schultheis Collection, Los Angeles Photographers Collection / Los Angeles Public Library.)

Within months of Roosevelt's declaration, oil production was ramped up in the nation's oil fields, including the Long Beach Field. Extraction rates, per the Maximum Efficient Rate Law, were established for fields that still flowed without the aid of pumps. Rates were not extended to fields that relied on pumps. It is hard to imagine the hysteria that gripped the nation in early 1942. On February 23, 1942, a Japanese submarine fired thirteen rounds of 5 1/2-inch shells at the Ellwood Refinery, just north of Santa Barbara. The news of the attack upset the nation as it was the first attack by a foreign power since the War of 1812. Besides these threats, German and Japanese submarines were exacting a horrific toll on merchant shipping. The SS *Larry Doheny*, a 66,000-barrel oil tanker owned by Los Angeles–based Richfield Oil, was sunk by a Japanese submarine off the California coast in December 1942.

Interestingly, oil production in the Signal Hill Field began to decline noticeably in the war years. The high point of production for the Field was reached in 1928, with the production of 60,854,191 barrels of oil that year. With the start of the Great Depression, oil

After decades of pumping oil in the Wilmington Oil Field, the land began to subside. The subsidence also impacted the Signal Hill oil field. This photograph, c. 1950s, was taken by Roger Coar, the longtime photographer for the Long Beach Press Telegram. While driving in the Long Beach Harbor area, Mr. Coar spotted this fire hydrant several feet above ground and thought it would be a better shot if his dog, King, was in the picture. He drove home and brought King back for this iconic photo. In the background, a naval warship can be seen. (Courtesy of Long Beach Press Telegram.)

production in Signal Hill in 1930 declined to 36,772,908 barrels. By the start of the war in 1941, production in Signal Hill had declined to 14,469,451 barrels. During the war, over 65.5 million barrels of oil were pumped in Signal Hill for both the war effort and for the home front.

With all of this demand, oil field subsidence problems started to appear at the end of the war in 1945. The nearby Wilmington Oil Field (southwest of Signal Hill, in Long Beach), which was discovered in 1932, began to collapse. The subsidence epicenter was the Long Beach Naval Shipyard, where building foundations cracked, and sewer and storm drain lines ruptured. In some areas, the subsidence was over twenty feet in depth. The Navy brought in landfill, raised foundations, and constructed dikes against the flooding ocean. A 1951 land survey showed that the base had sunk over two feet in one year. The naval base was not the only property impacted. Factories, docks, warehouses, and shipyards were sinking. Streets were buckling. The Commodore Heim Bridge tilted and the Long Beach City Hall moved three feet closer to the harbor. The second largest oil field in the nation was collapsing, and with it, the Signal Hill Field began to subside as well.

The subsidence caved in pipes or sheared them off. Of 160 wells surveyed in the Wilmington Oil Field, 96 were damaged, and 22 operators had to abandon their wells. Richfield Oil began to study the problem and in 1955 proposed injecting water under pressure into the Field. The pressurized water would push oil to areas of low pressure where wells could capture it. The pressurized water would also stop the subsidence. However, for the success of the "water flooding," the field would need to operate as one "unit." The Wilmington Field had thousands of separate owners and over one hundred separate operators. Under existing California law, the unit concept would not work.

Special legislation was proposed by the City of Long Beach in 1957. The City then held a referendum to amend their municipal charter; it was overwhelmingly approved. A special session of the legislature was called by Governor Goodwin J. Knight. The California Subsidence Act of 1958 was passed, and it provided for the pooling and unitization of the Field—first voluntary, and then compulsory if necessary. The Act contained rules for repressurizing the Field and for operational plans. The Act also mandated hearings and other protections for owners who might object to unitization. However, in 1956, the federal government had already moved in district court to force the City of Long Beach, the State of California, and the oil operators to immediately stop the subsidence at the Naval Shipyard and other government properties.

Eventually, over 21,600 acres were placed into the water flood area, including all of the Long Beach Harbor, south to Seal Beach and north to Lomita Avenue. The City of Long Beach committed to constructing the water infrastructure, with recovery of the costs through the sale of injection water. In what is known as "secondary recovery," oil and water is separated at centralized facilities. The process water is re-injected back into the field, and the oil is shipped to refineries. By late 1959 the subsidence had stopped, and by 1964 the Wilmington Field had produced over one billion barrels of oil. The Signal Hill Field would soon follow the water flooding model pioneered in the Wilmington Field. The Signal Hill Field would reach a total output of one billion barrels in 1985.[3]

As a young man, Jonathan Booth, like so many others, nurtured his own dream of discovering oil. He did not give up and eventually took action. In 1942, he raised money to redrill one of the wells on his father's property. The well produced forty barrels per day until the mid-1950s, and when production declined he finally had to abandon the well. He had no idea that secondary recovery would breathe new life into the oil field twenty years later.

Success Begins with a Plan

The secondary recovery effort in Signal Hill would not begin in earnest until 1968. However, the City needed a plan to counteract the declining production in the oil field and declining municipal revenues. The City's main source of revenue was from the oil barrel tax, which was falling as production tailed off. The City's incorporation as a "low property tax" city in 1924 would also play a crucial factor in the future land-use decisions.

Prior to the 1960s, Signal Hill, like many California cities, regulated land uses with their zoning ordinances. There was no comprehensive or master plan. With the rapid growth of the region during World War II and the "baby boom" of the 1950s, the state and larger cities began to consider drafting and adopting master plans, which would merge the many public infrastructure plans needed to operate a region or city into one comprehensive plan. In 1947, the state adopted a plan for the freeways in Los Angeles County to address regional traffic congestion. The larger cities of Los Angeles and Long Beach followed suit, adopting their own highway plans to deal with local traffic congestion. Cities then began to adopt park and recreation master plans. However, it was not until the late 1950s that the cities began to consider a wholistic approach, which would identify the issues facing a community and the strategies needed to overcome them.

It's also important to note that this was an era prior to California's landmark Proposition 13—adopted by the voters in 1978. Prior to 1978, all city councils could adjust their property tax revenues annually, without a vote of the people, to fund their municipal services. There has been much written about the "fiscalization of land uses," where cities compete for developments that generate as much revenue as

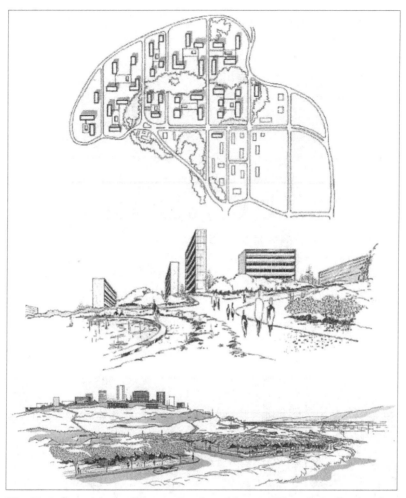

The City's first zoning ordinance was adopted in 1947. The urban planning firm of Simon Eisner & Associates was contracted to complete the City's first general plan, which was adopted in 1962. The plan recognized that Signal Hill had missed out on the considerable post–World War II population and construction boom. A comprehensive zoning ordinance and map were then adopted in 1964, allowing high-rise development on the Hilltop, up to eighty dwelling units per acre, with a six-story height limit. Below are original captions from the 1962 General Plan.

Top: "The plan of the high density area shows how each neighborhood complex has in its center a small plaza, play and quiet areas to help bring about a feeling of co-existence giving the individual a sense of security and identification." Middle: "Separation of pedestrian and vehicular traffic permits unobstructed movement between neighborhood high-rise apartment units." Bottom: "A panoramic view of the future skyline of Signal Hill as seen from Obispo Street." (Courtesy of City of Signal Hill.)

possible, with the least impact on city services. Proposition 13 turned local finances on their head; in many cases, residential development wound up generating less tax revenue than the municipal service costs. Before "Prop 13," cities did not worry about adding residences to their communities, since the city could adjust the property taxes to pay for the new services needed.

The City adopted its first general plan in 1962, and the plan identified the decline in oil production as a major issue confronting the City. The plan indicated that the recent decline in oil production was "causing the City to re-evaluate its long-range land-use policies and to consider alternate types of urban development." The general plan recognized that Signal Hill has missed out on the considerable post–World War II growth that fueled the development of the City of Lakewood and other nearby communities. In a short three-year period, 17,500 tract homes were constructed in Lakewood alone. Commercial development followed home construction, with the

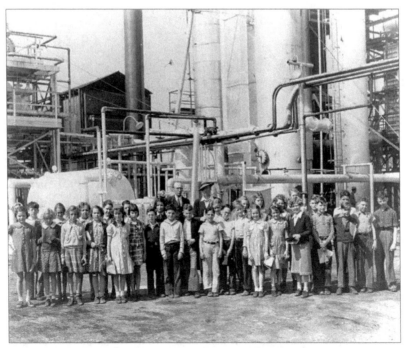

School children on a tour of an oil operation. Even while oil production was declining, it still played an important role in the life of the City of Signal Hill and its inhabitants. (Courtesy of City of Signal Hill.)

May Company department store opening in February 1952 in the Lakewood Mall, one of the nation's first master-planned shopping centers. The center parked 1,580 cars by 1954 and was the largest shopping center in the world. Signal Hill's leaders and residents could not have looked on without envy, as it seemed that the wave of development was about to pass them by. The City's general plan identified the need for a commercial town center at Willow Street and Cherry Avenue, along with other neighborhood commercial corridors. The plan also designed the Hilltop area for "high multiple residential development" at thirty-one to eighty families per acre. The plan illustrated stylized renderings of high-rise residential buildings to be constructed on the Hilltop area.

A section of the plan was devoted to discussing the oil industry. Notable in the document was the discussion of the declining oil reserves and the drop in property tax and petroleum revenues to the City. The plan stated that the majority of the decrease could be traced to the diminishing mineral value of the Field. The Los Angeles County Tax Assessor valued the Field's reserves at $23.1 million in 1950, and by 1960 the value of the Field had dropped to $11.2 million. In response to this decline, the general plan did not propose that the oil industry leave the community, but that the industry immediately undertake a general cleanup program and that the drilling operations be permitted under "regulated conditions consistent with the land-use districts in which they are located." The most far-reaching policy was that the surface area of land "no longer economically productive for oil extraction, be released for the long-range uses proposed in the plan." The plan concluded with the statement that it was unclear when oil extraction and production would be eliminated, so the timing of the redevelopment of the community was unknown.

As oil production continued to decline, the City commissioned an urban design study in 1970 that significantly intensified the proposed development for the Hilltop in the 1962 General Plan. The urban design plan included a community plaza and a community center building at the highest elevation. Clustered around the plaza were high-rise towers, consisting of residential units, restaurants, entertainment, commercial, and offices. The urban designers envisioned parking structures serving a "city on the Hill," with pedestrian bridges, escalators, water features, and green spaces. The plan relied on "modern architecture" similar to the Los Angeles Music Center. The designers wrote that "Potentially, Signal Hill could assume an image of world-wide significance" and recommended a planning and design committee to coordinate and review all Hilltop development. That plan was never implemented.

It is perhaps easy in hindsight to see that the 1962 General Plan was a vision for the Hilltop that could never have been built. The plan was developed in an era prior to the marriage of economic viability with land use planning. The City would struggle for the next thirty years with what type of land uses made sense on the declining oil field, not just on the Hilltop. Meanwhile in the 1960s environmental planning was coming of age.[4]

> The City and oil companies weren't the only ones taking, or trying to take, action. In the early 1970s, Jonathan Booth was able to have his well at the northwest corner of Redondo Avenue and Pacific Coast Highway removed. He graded the land and constructed a Jack in the Box restaurant. Life moves on.

The Right Way to Extract Oil

Based on the Wilmington Oil Field's success in injecting water into the oil deposits, the Signal Hill Field was divided by Texaco, Shell, and ARCO into three operating units for the purposes of managing the secondary recovery system. Texaco initiated a pilot project in order to test the feasibility of flooding and secondary recovery in the Field. The project was located on the Field lease, near the intersection of Spring Street and Atlantic Avenue. This location would eventually become one of the several centralized drill sites, where the City and the oil operators hoped to concentrate drilling operations to free up land for redevelopment.

The first injection well, Field 36, was drilled to 5,160 feet and began injecting 1,500 barrels of water per day at 1,000 psi. The California Division of Oil and Gas (DOG) reported that within thirty days, production in the first affected well had doubled, and it had tripled by September. With the success of the pilot program, the oil companies began the detailed planning for the secondary recovery system. Just like the Wilmington Field, state legislation was necessary to establish the Signal Hill operating units. This legislation was sponsored by Signal Hill's then assembly member, George Deukmejian, who would go on to become the 35th governor of California. The unit operators were responsible for dispersing revenues to many property owners whose mineral and surface rights had been consolidated into the various operating units.

The construction of the secondary recovery system was no small feat and was not completed until 1971. It included extending water pipes to support the water flood injection wells, and the installation of pipes to collect oil, natural gas, and water pumped out of the Field. Of the total returned mixture, approximately 10% was oil and gas, while 90% was water, which was then reinjected back into the field. The project also involved the construction of plants to separate the gas and oil from the returned injection water. Also necessary, was placing a new 660KV wiring system underground to supply energy to the Field to operate the water flooding system and the wells. The gas collection system made a substantial improvement in the local air quality, as diesel electric generators were eliminated at the wells and the natural gas was collected at the wellhead, instead of being vented into the atmosphere. The project involved the abandonment of some wells and the re-drilling of others.

DOG records document that over 2.1 million barrels of water had been injected by the beginning of 1968 just for the pilot program. On November 1, 1971, the Signal Hill Field West Unit was created. Two other units would come into production, the Central Unit and the East Unit. The West Unit included 229 owners: from large companies like Texaco and Shell Oil, dozens of smaller operators, and hundreds of small owners. Atlantic Richfield formed the Signal Hill Central Unit in December of 1971, and Texaco formed the West Unit in 1972. Later analysis of oil field operations revealed that the water flooding was too rapid and employed too much water. By the early 1970s, the United States imported 35% of its oil from foreign sources. In October 1973, the Organization of Arab Petroleum Exporting Countries imposed an oil embargo against the United States for supporting Israel during the Yom Kippur

War. The reinvestment in the Signal Hill Field had seemed to come at an opportune time.[5]

Shell Leads the Way

Shell became a pioneer in the construction and operation of secondary oil recovery systems in the late 1950s, having been an early player in the Signal Hill Field. Royal Dutch Shell first began selling gasoline in the United States in 1921—gasoline imported from the Dutch colony of Sumatra. Wanting to compete with Standard Oil to take advantage of the growing car market, Shell began investing in California exploration. Shell's investment in the Discovery Well and in the Signal Hill Field provided the company with ability to serve the growing Los Angeles market, and by 1922 Shell had merged with Union Oil Company, developing a nationwide network of service stations and refineries. Shell developed many innovations, including the first 100-octane gasoline for airplanes. The oil from the Signal Hill Field was well suited to the manufacture of aviation gas, and Shell began selling fuel to the US Army Air Corps in 1934. Shell shared its technological developments with other oil companies as more aviation fuel was required during World War II than Shell could produce. Later, in the 1950s, Shell would pioneer the development of jet fuels and unleaded gasoline.

Shell Oil, Texaco, and Atlantic Richfield would go on to invest untold millions of dollars into extending the life of the Signal Hill Field. No one at that time could have foreseen that the major oil companies would begin to sell off their facilities and mineral rights over the course of only a few years, changing the destiny of Signal Hill and the oil field. Other forces would come to impact these major decisions, including a growing interest by the public in improving the natural environment.[6]

VI

The Tipping Point: January 28, 1969

The Congress, the Administration and the public all share a
profound commitment to the rescue of our natural environment,
and the preservation of the Earth as a place
both habitable by and hospitable to man.

—President Richard Nixon,
message to Congress about establishing the EPA

Silent Spring, published in 1962, was Rachel Carson's fourth and most pointed book on the environment. In it she spoke of the choice the world was facing: "We stand now where two roads diverge. But unlike the roads in Robert Frost's familiar poem, they are not equally fair." With this, she warned about the overuse of synthetic chemical pesticides that had grown after World War II. Since these pesticides were primarily petroleum based, she was attacked as an alarmist by industry and some in government. Rare for a woman in her day, she graduated with a master's degree in zoology from Johns Hopkins University in 1932. During the Great Depression she worked for the US Bureau of Fisheries and became the chief editor of all of the Bureau's publications. In 1941, 1952, and 1955, she published books about the ocean.

The release of *Silent Spring* can be traced to the beginning of a growing environmental movement. Testifying before Congress in

1963, Carson warned of human health effects and the impacts on the environment of the overuse of pesticides. "The road we have long been traveling is deceptively easy, a smooth superhighway on which we progress with great speed, but at its end lies disaster." She would not live to see the environmental movement take shape, passing away in 1964 after a long battle with breast cancer. However, in early 1969 the environmental movement would suddenly take off. It was then that there began to be hope for humanity to make the right choice: "The other fork of the road—the one less traveled by—offers our last, our only chance to reach a destination that assures the preservation of the earth."[1]

The Loss of a Few Birds

On January 28, 1969, an offshore drilling rig operated by Union Oil experienced an underwater blowout. While changing out pipe, an insufficient amount of drilling mud was forced into the hole. An extreme amount of natural gas blew out the mud, split the casing, and cracked the ocean bottom in the vicinity of the well. The oil spilled out for eleven days, since the technology to control underwater blowouts was nonexistent. Over three million gallons of oil spilled, polluting over thirty-five miles of Pacific Coast beaches. It was an environmental catastrophe, with over 3,600 dead seabirds inventoried by cleanup teams, and there were large numbers of dead seals and dolphins. The spill claimed uncounted fish and invertebrates, ruined kelp forests, and impacted endangered bird species.

Union Oil President Fred Hartley stated, "I don't like to call it a disaster, because there has been no loss of human life. I am amazed at the publicity for the loss of a few birds." The public reaction against the oil companies involved in the spill was immediate. President Nixon flew out from Washington, DC, to view the damage, noting: "It is sad that it was necessary that Santa Barbara should be the example that had to bring it to the attention of the American people. . . . The Santa Barbara incident has frankly touched the conscience of the American people." Thomas Storke, the editor of the *Santa Barbara News-Press,* commented that never in his long life had he seen

The oil platform responsible for the 1969 Santa Barbara oil spill. (Wikimedia Commons, public domain.)

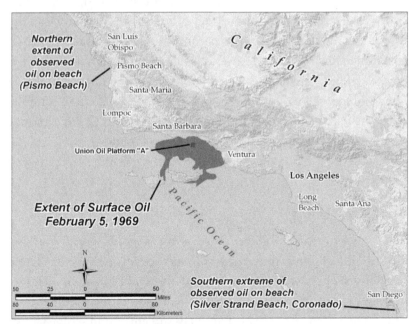

The extent of the 1969 oil spill, which sent oil as far north as Pismo Beach and as far south as San Diego. (Wikimedia Commons, public domain.)

such an aroused populace at the grassroots. "This oil pollution has done something I have never seen before in Santa Barbara—it has united citizens of all political persuasions in a truly nonpartisan cause." The first Earth Day would be held April 22, 1970.[2]

A New Direction, and No Turning Back

When one thinks of environmental activists, the name Richard Nixon is not the first to come up. However, the 37th president is arguably the greatest of our nation's environmental presidents. Congress had been working on a national environmental policy; most notably, Washington (State) Senator Henry "Scoop" Jackson had introduced legislation in 1967 calling for the National Environmental Policy Act (NEPA). The public outrage from the Santa Barbara oil spill came at a time when Congress was considering NEPA. Also, in 1969, the Cuyahoga River was so polluted it caught fire, for the thirteenth time since 1868. Congress passed and President Nixon signed NEPA into law in January 1970. The Environmental Protection Agency was formed later that year.

Nixon then signed the Clean Air Act in 1970; the Marine Protection, Research and Sanctuaries Act of 1972; and the Safe Drinking Water Act in 1974. These acts became the cornerstone of federal activism in environmental issues. The legislation was not just limited to the federal level. The State of California adopted the California Environmental Quality Act in 1970. The California Coastal Commission was then created by statewide initiative in 1972. The State Lands Commission banned offshore drilling for seventeen years. Federal and state laws regulating oil drilling were overhauled. Clearly, the times were changing.

Never by Chance

In a 1974 letter from California Governor Ronald Reagan marking Signal Hill's fiftieth anniversary of cityhood, he observed, "These past fifty exciting years have witnessed the evolution of an oil boom town into an outstanding example of living and industry compatibility. I share with you the pride felt today and am confident the City of Signal Hill will continue to provide its citizens with the very best in leadership and community facilities that make it a wonderful place in which to live and work."

The year of 1974 would become a pivotal year in Signal Hill's history. As the City celebrated its Golden Anniversary of incorporation, the city's leaders were struggling financially with the decline in the oil-field production and the commensurate decline in revenues to fund city operations and capital projects. Even prior to 1974, City services were under siege. The aftermath of the Hancock oil refinery fire in 1958 resulted in the city council disbanding the city's small fire department. The fire had burned for three days, and it was necessary to call on the County of Los Angeles Fire Department, the City of Long Beach Fire Department, the City of Vernon, and the local air force base at Long Beach Airport to assist the City's small department in controlling the inferno.

We live in an era where public safety departments have entered into automatic and mutual aid agreements, so we have become accustomed to public safety agencies responding to help one another deal with major public safety incidents. However, this was not the case

Oil would always be a risky business. On May 22, 1958, the Hancock Refinery erupted in flames, killing two workers, and causing millions in damage during the following three days in which it burned. Jonathan Booth had been working for Hancock Oil since just after the war. He was away making a sales call to Proctor & Gamble in East Los Angeles that day, and could see the fire "back home," but didn't know what was happening. (Courtesy of City of Signal Hill.)

in 1958. An outcome of the Hancock Refinery Fire was city council's voting to annex into the Los Angeles County Fire Protection District in 1968 in order to provide improved fire protection to the community. This annexation resulted in a savings to the City's budget, as the annual costs of providing fire protection would now be paid by property taxes through a special district tax. However, after the passage of California's landmark tax limitation voter initiative—Proposition 13 in 1978—future city councils would be prohibited from shifting the costs of services onto the property tax bill without a vote of the people.

In 1974, the City continued to operate its own police department, and it was proud to have its own city library. But, all of this came at a cost to the small, low property tax city. Then–Mayor Keyton King, Vice Mayor Gertrude Beebe, and Council members Ennis Neff, William Mendenhall, and Nick Mekis had quite the task before them. After a series of contentious public hearings, in 1974 the council formed the Signal Hill Redevelopment Agency, with the express goal of spurring economic development to find replacement revenues for the declining oil field revenues. This was not an action taken lightly or popular with landowners. Redevelopment agencies had the power to take property against the wishes of landowners. Known as "eminent domain," the concept had its roots in English law, where the sovereign could take land for the construction of public roads. The right is also contained in the US Constitution and requires just compensation for the taking of land. The Agency's boundaries included only the oil field and shied away from established residential areas.

After serving their terms, King, Neff, and Mekis had a chance to reflect on their actions to form the Signal Hill Redevelopment Agency in 1974. They recalled vividly the 1973–1974 oil embargo, which was imposed on the United States by the Arab members of the Organization of Petroleum Exporting Countries (OPEC) during the 1973 Arab–Israeli War. The embargo created havoc in the US economy, resulting in gasoline rationing and long lines at gas stations. Gasoline prices increased overnight from an average of 38 cents per gallon to 84 cents per gallon. Odd-even rationing was instituted, whereby gas for private vehicles could be purchased on alternating days, with the day determined by the last digit—odd or even—in the license plate. Beside resulting in higher fuel prices and rationing, the embargo had a series of regulatory effects: the national vehicular speed limit was lowered to 55 mile per hour, vehicle fuel efficiency and energy conservation standards were first established, and there was a national push to develop domestic energy sources.

The former City leaders also remembered their discussing how the nation was concerned with the contradictory goals of increasing the national production of oil and of preserving the environment. They thought that with the water flooding and the unitization of the oil field by the major oil companies, Signal Hill was assisting the nation in dealing with the embargo, much like during World War II. They also noted the many activities involved in unitization, such as removing the derricks, undergrounding the electrical wires in the oil field and installing an underground electrical backbone system to serve the oil pumps, installing landscaping on the oil field, and capturing the natural gas at the wellheads through piping instead of burning it into the atmosphere, which amounted to improving the environment for all. They recalled how they believed the oil companies were implementing long-overdue environmental improvements. They were rightfully proud of the progress that the City was making.[3]

Signal Hill Confronts the Region's Resource Limitations and Pollution

The explosive regional population and industrial growth during World War II followed by the postwar economic boom forced local governments to face the region's resource limitations as well as the pollution plaguing the area. As early as 1905, there was growing concern by the City of Los Angeles over the lack of water supply needed to support urban development. The City proposed a bold project of capturing water in the Owens Valley adjacent to the eastern Sierra Nevada mountain range and piping it to the city, traveling over 233 miles. After eight years of construction, on November 5, 1913, the spigot on the Los Angeles Aqueduct was opened, and Chief Engineer William Mulholland declared, "There it is—take it!" Reportedly,

43,000 Angelenos watched water pour into the municipal water system just north of the city of San Fernando.

The pressure on Signal Hill's resources began in the 1940s. Air pollution from the oil industry impacted Signal Hill, but also, it impacted the region's air pollution. At a time when each home had a backyard incinerator to burn refuse, thousands of backyard incinerators fouled the air as well. Plus, Signal Hill's municipal incinerator—burning commercial refuse—added to air quality problems. Drinking water aquifers became polluted from septic tanks, and the City's local sewage treatment plant became unusable. Flood waters and urban runoff from the oil field polluted the local streams and flood control channels. Signal Hill needed to join with other cities and form special utility agencies to deal with the challenges facing the community and the region.[4]

Controlling the Impacts of Air Pollution

Signal Hill, like many communities, collected refuse and incinerated it for decades. Then, smog and air pollution became a regional issue, and the City's incinerator was shuttered in the 1960s and demolished

in 1978. The region's topography, wind patterns, and sunshine created the natural conditions that induced smog and air pollution. In July 1943, Los Angeles had the first of many bad smog days as a result of growing pollution from war-time industries, more vehicles on the region's roads, and dozens of other sources of air pollution—including the oil refineries and the oil fields. Visibility in downtown Los Angeles that July was reported to be only three blocks. Residents reported that the air smelled like bleach, their eyes stung, and their noses

The City operated both a local refuse incinerator and had its own refuse trucks. Pictured here is the City's refuse incinerator shortly after it closed in the 1960s. (Courtesy City of Signal Hill.)

City public works staff display some of their trucks and other equipment, including an asphalt roller, c. 1940s. (Courtesy of City of Signal Hill.)

ran. Similar smog plagued Los Angeles the next summer. Angelenos watched in horror as twenty people died in 1948 from a smog incident in Donora, Pennsylvania, where half the town also grew sick. Thousands died in the London Great Smog of 1952. No one really knew the source of the smog nor how to stop it.

Homes since the 1910s were routinely constructed with backyard incinerators, of which there were over 300,000 in Los Angeles County alone by 1947. Air pollution had grown to be so bad that the board of supervisors established the nation's first air pollution authority, the Los Angeles County Air Pollution Control District, in 1947. The recommendation to form the district came from noted pollution expert Raymond Tucker, who had been hired by the *Los Angeles Times* in 1946 to study the region's air pollution problems and to propose solutions. Tucker's twenty-three recommendations were vigorously opposed by the LA Chamber of Commerce and oil companies. However, the board went on to follow up on the local ordinance by drafting state legislation to allow counties to set up air pollution control districts. Air pollution was so bad that the bill was virtually unopposed in the state legislature and was signed into law by Governor Earl Warren in October 1947, putting teeth into the pollution reduction program.

Highland Park Optimist Club banquet, with attendees wearing smog gas masks, 1954. (Los Angeles Daily News Negative Archive (Collection 1387). UCLA Library Special Collections, Charles E. Young Research Library, UCLA.)

Soon after, burning refuse at dumps was prohibited, and backyard incinerators were banned in 1958. Cities like Signal Hill began to pick up all refuse and burn it in local incinerators. The public was reluctant to give up the incinerators and blamed the oil refineries for smog. They were indeed partly to blame. Regulators noted that large amounts of gasoline escaped from storage tanks—up to 120,000 gallons per day in the region. The air pollution district began to require controls on the storage tanks to prevent gas from escaping. Eventually, controls were extended to gasoline service stations, and in 1978, gasoline dispensing nozzles were required to have a second vapor recovery hose. As the water flooding and secondary recovery system was being installed in the Signal Hill oil field, well-head gas was being captured, pumped to a central gas processing plant, and purchased by the Long Beach Gas Company.

Local politicians began to see air pollution as a much larger issue, not just confined to Los Angeles County. There was an effort to form a multi-county air pollution authority, but Governor Ronald Reagan vetoed legislative efforts. It was not until Governor Jerry Brown was elected that the South Coast Air Quality Management District was formed and become effective on January 1, 1977.[5]

A Victory for the Environment and a Victory for the Taxpayers

With the intervention of federal authorities, the region was well on its way to controlling the massive flooding that inundated the region after the 1934 winter storms. The regional and local flood control system served Signal Hill as intended, capturing runoff and moving it efficiently out to the ocean to prevent flooding and loss of life. Unfortunately, another, more vexing, problem was awaiting Signal Hill—deteriorating groundwater and surface-water quality. Signal Hill constructed a wastewater treatment plant and local sewer system in the 1920s to deal with the groundwater contamination problem. Homes and businesses were removed from their septic systems.

Small municipal wastewater systems, however, were becoming more expensive and complex to operate over time, especially as petroleum and industrial uses covered over fifty percent of Signal Hill's land mass. Several Los Angeles County cities moved forward in 1923 with special legislation to form the Los Angeles County Sanitation Districts. The districts were envisioned as a

Signal Hill's municipal sewage treatment plant, c. 1930s. As the community grew, the City constructed and operated its own activated sludge plant. Signal Hill was included in District #3, with the City of Long Beach, when the Los Angeles County Sanitation Districts were formed in 1923. However, a large part of Long Beach was sewered to a screening plant at the Long Beach Harbor entrance and to County Sanitation District trunk sewer lines. Sewers were not extended into Signal Hill until the 1960s. (Courtesy of City of Signal Hill.)

regional wastewater utility that would eventually own and operate miles of trunk-line sewers and wastewater plants. By 1949, the districts expanded their services to cover refuse, as incinerators were becoming an air quality issue. The districts eventually grew to one of the nation's largest wastewater and refuse utilities, serving seventy-seven cities, with sixteen service areas, and serving 5.6 million people in Los Angeles County today.

The Federal Water Pollution Control Act of 1948 was one of the first US laws to address water pollution, primarily working with wastewater treatment throughout the nation to deal with water pollution. Groundwater pollution was such an issue that, after Signal Hill purchased the water system from the City of Long Beach in the 1920s, the City moved to close the municipal water wells located in the community, preferring to drill new water wells far north into the City of Long Beach, miles from the main Reservoir Park water storage and treatment facility. The City also eventually abandoned its wastewater treatment plant and joined the Los Angeles County Sanitation Districts, as District No. 29. Signal Hill became one of the few districts that was not combined with other surrounding communities, in recognition of its unique wastewater needs. The District provided the major trunk-line sewers and sewage treatment plants, while the local sewer lines were owned and maintained by the City. The Signal Hill property owners approved District 29's taking over the ownership and maintenance responsibility for the local sewers in 2002.

Mayor Thomas Denham is being held by Sergeant Art LeBlanc, while council member William Mendenhall looks on, as the city ceremonially turns the valve connecting the city's sewer system to the Los Angeles County Sanitation Districts in April 1964. The City would shutter its sewer treatment plant when it joined the regional sewage treatment organization. (Courtesy of City of Signal Hill.)

While the community's wastewater issues were being

handled by the County Sanitation Districts, Signal Hill and other communities continued to struggle with surface-water contamination issues. Water pollution in streams, rivers, lakes, and bays was a growing problem in the 1960s. Even though the days were long gone where oil flowed in earthen ditches downhill to the refineries, there were substantial pollutants—traveling into the local streams when it rained—from roads and urban land uses. There was no regional utility dedicated to dealing with treating surface-water pollution, as was the case with the County Sanitation Districts, and the flood control system did not filter out pollutants as rainwater was rushed out of Signal Hill to the Los Angeles River and onto the Los Cerritos flood control channel.

The Federal Water Pollution Control Act Amendments of 1972, the Clean Water Act of 1977, and the Water Quality Act of 1987 were all intended to address water quality issues with goals including providing "fishable" and "swimmable" waters wherever attainable and restoring the chemical and biological integrity of the nation's waters. The Clean Water Act in 1972 established a stormwater permit, which cities had to obtain in order to discharge water from their storm drains into federally protected waterways. The first of the stormwater discharge permits were issued to Los Angeles County and its cities in 1991, and contained simple-to-follow programs, such as street sweeping and public education programs. By giving the public litigation rights in the Clean Water Act, Congress empowered everyday citizens to enforce water quality standards, significantly upping the ante for communities found out of compliance.

A major change occurred when the Los Angeles Regional Water Quality Control Board issued the 2001 regional stormwater permit. The permit was altered from the prior permit's basic programs—like vacuuming streets with sweepers, public education, and restaurant inspections—to requiring that cities take water quality samples, where compliance was tied to meeting stringent water-quality standards. The water-quality standards dated from the 1970s and required serious revisions. Later studies revealed that the water quality standards were overly protective and could be revised without harming the environment. Just as Jessie Nelson stepped forward

The excavation and stormwater chambers for the stormwater capture project at the Long Beach Airport, located at the southeastern end of the airport. After completion of the chambers in April 2018, the excavation was then backfilled with earth. The project was designed to assist Long Beach, Signal Hill, Lakewood, and the Long Beach Airport to comply with federal surface-water quality requirements that protect the Los Cerritos Channel. The $22.7 million project was entirely grant-funded with $15.2 million in Caltrans monies and $7.5 million contributed from the County Flood Control District. The project diverts runoff from the channel to the buried cisterns, where the water then percolates into the ground. This was the first of two stormwater capture projects funded statewide by Caltrans working with local cities. (Courtesy of Richard Watson & Associates.)

into the controversies over city incorporation decades ago, Signal Hill Mayor and Council member Larry Forester stepped forward into the controversies surrounding storm water.

Forester grew up in post–World War II Long Island. The oldest of six children born to devout Catholic parents, he attended parochial school and explained that there was no doubt that he would attend Notre Dame for college. He received a bachelor's degree in engineering and went on to receive a master's degree in ocean engineering from Catholic University. These would turn out to be the perfect degrees for helping provide leadership to the City and the region in the complicated technical requirements of storm-water treatment. Working for Exxon, he traveled the country, ending up in San Francisco in 1970s. He moved to Signal Hill in 1987 and became active in local politics. In 1999, he was appointed to a vacant city council seat. When his terms was up, he ran for office, was elected, and ended up serving for another twenty years.

He put his degrees to good use, leading a coalition of forty-eight cities known as the Coalition for Practical Regulation. The cities attempted to make sense of the new requirements of the 2001 storm-water permit. Forester joined a group of regional leaders and engineers in May 2003 at a symposium of the American Society of Civil Engineers, immersing himself in the storm-water requirements and proposing solutions. This was a time of great uncertainty, since cities did not have storm water utilities, and they had no dedicated funding source to pay for the new permit requirements. Signal Hill, one of the smallest cities in Los Angeles County, stepped forward to bring together a regional effort to educate the cities and propose funding options. The City coordinated an economic impact study by the University of Southern California, which concluded that the costs of the full treatment of storm water in the region could range from $43.7 billion to $283.9 billion depending on how large of a storm event the cities were required to capture and treat. During this time, Forester led the effort to revise several standards—including those for trash and metals in storm water. The Coalition also coordinated several lawsuits against the new regulations, attempting to make them more reasonable. The group prevailed against the 2001 permit, forcing the regional board back to the drawing board to design a permit that would improve water quality but recognize the cost burden on the cities. The regional board did not reissue the regional storm-water permit until 2012. This permit was also litigated, and it was overturned in 2019. The City led a regional effort of thirty-seven cities, including the City of Los Angeles and other Los Angeles County cities, to complete scientific studies on the Los Angeles and San Gabriel Rivers, resulting in revisions to the water quality standards for copper and lead. These scientific efforts are continuing into the foreseeable future.

Forester encouraged the city to comply with the storm-water permit and the property owners approved of a fee to fund the removal of trash found in storm water in 2002. In 2005, Forester pushed for state legislation, AB 2554, to assist the County Flood Control District in levying a fee for storm-water programs. He pushed for a local share of the revenues in AB 2554, so that the cities would have a guaranteed amount of revenue to implement storm-water improvements. In 2011 and 2012, the City worked with the County on a regional fee. Known as the Clean Water Clean Beaches Measure, the funding measure was ultimately tabled by the board of supervisors that year. Undeterred, Forester organized elected officials from the League of California Cities and the California Contract Cities Association to propose funding options. The group issued a report with forty separate recommendations analyzing where the Clean Water Clean Beaches Measure fell short, and it concluded with the need to reintroduce a regional fee.

The City worked with the regional board on the 2012 storm-water permit to institute a storm-water planning process for local government, where cities could work in groups to build projects that improve water quality. In 2017, Forester and the group of elected officials began working with the County on a second attempt at the regional fee. Known as Measure W, the property tax measure was approved by the County's voters in the November 2018 statewide election. The parcel tax is estimated to collect $300 million annually for projects that improve water quality and capture storm water for reuse. Forester was very proud of a $9 million Caltrans grant received by the City to construct a major storm-water capture project at the south end of the Long Beach Airport, which would help Signal Hill, the City of Long Beach, and the airport improve water quality and provide additional groundwater for the region.

What makes these accomplishments even more remarkable is that Forester was diagnosed with HIV in 1985. He began working in AIDS-related causes when he moved to Signal Hill in 1987. By 1994, he was diagnosed with AIDs, and he began a course of triple drug therapy. He suffered from severe bouts of the illness, and he was not sure he had the energy to serve on the city council, much less the effort needed to lead the forty-eight city coalition. As Forester was getting ready to step off the city council in March 2019, he was rightfully proud of his efforts to find a permanent funding solution to improve water quality and of his pursuit of improved science. He felt that this was one of his greatest public service accomplishments. It was a victory for the environment and a victory for the taxpayers.[6]

After All, Signal Hill Is Also . . . a Hill!

The Hill had offered some amusement to the oil-field workers and residents even prior to the incorporation of the City in 1924. It rises 392 feet above sea level, and many of the direct approaches to the summit were short and steep. Hill Street was like a roller coaster, following the terrain to the summit, with short stretches steeper than a 15% grade. Some of the earliest local car owners and oil-field workers—nearly all with Model Ts, of course—began trying to conquer Hill Street, but the T's 22 horsepower motor proved unequal to the steep, rutted dirt road. From the 1950s into the 1970s, the Signal Hill Chamber of Commerce recreated the challenge, inviting Model T enthusiasts to give it a try. With a paved road—and

The Long Beach Model T Club resurrected the Model T Hill Climb from 1957 through 1977; pictured is a re-enactor on Hill Street in 1961. The original hill climb started in the 1920s, soon after the discovery of oil in Signal Hill. The Model T did not have a fuel pump and relied on gravity to feed gasoline to the carburetor. The driver either had to have a full tank of gas to make it to the top of Hill Street, or needed to drive the car in reverse. (Courtesy of City of Signal Hill.)

sometimes driving backwards to take advantage of the low-torque reverse gear—many of them succeeded.

Later, in the 1970s, with the derricks gone and open land still available, thrill-seekers began using the hill in the other direction. The earliest serious skateboard enthusiasts were from the surfing community, and for the surfers around Long Beach, the city on top of the hill shone like a beacon. Plus, there was plenty of room for spectators as there was very little development around Hill Street at that time. The world's first skateboard competition, suggested by ABC TV and the "Guinness Book of World Records" program, had participants flying down the steepest part of Hill Street in 1975. The winner topped 50 mph, and later modifications to board design raised even that seemingly insane speed. The Signal Hill Redevelopment Agency underwrote a documentary film in 2013, *The Signal Hill Speed Run*, that details the history of the event. The Speed Run and its keg-party atmosphere became famous in boarding circles, touted in ads for skateboard companies.

Not surprisingly, injuries—some serious—occurred. The assistant city manager at the time, Jerry Caton, who went on to become

An aerial photograph of Signal Hill in the 1980s. Hill Street, site of 1970s skateboard competitions, can be seen running off this photo near its bottom left corner. (Courtesy of City of Signal Hill.)

the long-time city manager of the City of Downey, remarked that the races ended over liability issues. Although the race was held in Signal Hill, contestants came to their untimely stops in the City of Long Beach, which was not amused as the insurance claims began to pile up. The merriment ended with the fourth annual race.

The Signal Hill Speed Run is considered the first extreme sporting event. Extreme sporting has since gone mainstream, including recognition in the Olympics. Today, several favorite bicycling, running, walking and hiking routes take advantage of Signal Hills's aerobic possibilities, albeit in a safer manner.

Promotional poster for the City's 2013 documentary film.

VII

"A Good, Modern Town When the Derricks are Gone"

*"From a community covered by hundreds of oil derricks in the
1930s and 1940s to the pleasant, distinctive gem it is today,
is truly an amazing accomplishment."*
—Lori Woods, Signal Hill council member, April 19, 2014

Signal Hill was at a major crossroads at the beginning of the 1970s.
No longer able to survive on oil field revenues, given the decline in
production, the City needed sustainable long-term alternative revenues. The City's Achilles Heel was its incorporation in 1924 as a "low
property tax city," surrendering almost the entire share of local property tax revenues to Los Angeles County. Perhaps the original City
founders either could not or did not foresee that oil field production
would naturally decline and along with it the fortunes of the City.
The decline in production continued even with the reinvestment in
the field by Shell Oil, ARCO, and Texaco in the secondary recovery
process in the 1970s. The major oil companies would begin their disinvestment from Signal Hill in 1984 and would be totally gone from
the City by 1999.

However, the City slowly and methodically turned itself around
with the vision, courage, and hard work of elected officials, the
involvement of an energized populace, and the assistance of a cadre
of talented staff. A significant contributor to this renaissance was the

An aerial photograph of Signal Hill in the 1980s, while derricks were being taken down and the land was starting to be repurposed and redeveloped. Some described Signal Hill at this stage as a "layer cake." It is obvious here how it had been a hill that was then was completely "graded out" for oil. Note also how the hill is surrounded by industrial spaces. (Courtesy of City of Signal Hill.)

Signal Hill Redevelopment Agency (SHRDA), which operated for thirty-seven years. Governor Jerry Brown, in his search for revenues to fix the State's chronically unbalanced budgets, terminated all of the State's 400-plus redevelopment agencies in 2011, with assistance from the state legislature.

When the SHRDA closed its books that March, the community had—in under four decades—accomplished what seemed to be a miraculous turnaround. In total, the SHRDA had invested over $102 million back into improving the community in various ways. It had financed construction for major infrastructure improvements, like Cherry Avenue and Spring Street. It had enabled construction of essential buildings, like the police station and the Signal Hill Library. It had subsidized the construction of over 320 units of housing for moderate and low income families, as well as special needs individuals, leaving a legacy of 248 low and very low income units in well-managed developments. Signal Hill had now become a community where both people and business wanted to take root and thrive.

Beginning the Difficult Task of Reclaiming Signal Hill

The history of redevelopment agencies in California dates to the Community Redevelopment Act in 1945. Most early redevelopment agencies relied on federal funds until the state's voters approved Proposition 18 in 1952. Proposition 18 established "tax increment financing" to deal with blighted areas of communities. Redevelopment agencies would adopt a project area and calculate all property taxes from the area, including tax revenues received by the local schools and the county. This calculation would become the "base year" and was "frozen." The redevelopment agency then invested in improving the area and attracting new development, and the property tax revenues would increase. The redevelopment agency would capture all the increased property tax revenues from all the taxing entities from the base year and continue the cycle of reinvestment.

In theory, the tax increment was a powerful financial tool; however, redevelopment agencies were slow to form since taxing entities did not agree to freezing their property tax revenues. Agency areas

This map illustrates the difficulty of developing in the Signal Hill oil field. Just dealing with the number of active wells (+) and inactive wells (.) requiring abandonment was a massive undertaking. The wells were documented by the Signal Hill Redevelopment Agency when it began the task of purchasing the town lots in the former Windemere Tract in order to combine the lots into larger parcels for proper development. The SHRDA assisted in the construction of the A&A Concrete plant, the EDCO Headquarters, and EDCO Transfer Station. The SHRDA would, over time, invest more than $40.3 million in purchasing the town lots. (Courtesy of City of Signal Hill.)

A portion of Signal Hill in the 1980s, after the derricks had been removed, being prepared for new residential and commercial uses. (Courtesy of City of Signal Hill.)

were small in size in the 1940s through the 1960s, since tax revenues were being shifted from one taxing entity to another, limiting agency formation. Long Beach formed their redevelopment agency in 1964. There were only twenty-seven project areas in California as of 1966, with the largest being one hundred acres in size.

Long-term and sustainable financing for agencies did not really take hold until SB 90 was passed in 1972. This bill guaranteed that the State would keep school districts whole from their property tax losses that were taken by redevelopment agencies. This one change resulted in the formation of another 202 redevelopment agencies by 1976, with the Signal Hill Redevelopment Agency (SHRDA) being formed in 1974 to replace declining oil field revenues.

The SHRDA territory comprised 840 acres of former oil fields. The boundaries were carefully drawn to avoid existing residential and commercial areas. The City of Signal Hill had also begun the difficult task of resolving petroleum's legacy issues—the town lot drilling, the environmental cleanup of soils, the mitigation of improperly abandoned oil wells, and the removal of obsolete pipe-lines and tanks—with the involvement of the SHRDA. Well aban-donments were a serious challenge, with some owners just walking away and leaving their environmental liability behind.

The success of the SHRDA in finding new sources of revenue as the oil boom declined is only part of the story of reclaiming Sig-nal Hill. Signal Hill Petroleum invested in the community, as they developed new technologies to tease more oil from the land. An involved citizenry and engaged civic leaders continued to guide the City through the ever-shifting landscape of politics, money, and demographics, enacting development moratoriums to prevent uncontrolled growth, revising the general plan twice, and repeatedly tweaking details of the process.[1]

New Life for the Signal Hill Oil Field

The Barto Company was formed in 1979 and focused on commer-cial and residential development in Southern California. Founded by Jerry Barto, the company would work with the City to resolve the complexities of continuing successful oil field operations, while freeing up land for redevelopment. The Barto Company's first foray into developing an oil field occurred with their acquisition of the West Newport Oil Field, located in Costa Mesa, for residential and commercial development. This acquisition resulted in the company sensing an opportunity in nearby Signal Hill. Worldwide geopoliti-cal events would create an opportunity for the Barto Company and Signal Hill Petroleum.

Shell Oil Company began to encounter social problems and intensified environmental pressure in the mid-1980s, with boycotts of their products due to their investments in South Africa. Picketing in US cities began to adversely impact Shell's gasoline sales. Shell then encountered soil contamination, with $240 million in soil cleanup costs, at the Rocky Mountain Arsenal in Colorado. Working with the military, Shell had developed nerve gas there during World War II. The State of Colorado sued Shell and the US Army in 1989, under the newly enacted federal Superfund program, to force a cleanup of the site. Shell began to look elsewhere for oil supplies and settled on the Gulf of Mexico. Signal Hill Petroleum was founded in 1984 when the Barto Company acquired the Shell land holdings and oil leases in Signal Hill. In 1989, Signal Hill Petroleum purchased the ARCO East Unit interest and operatorship from ARCO.

Texaco's holdings in Signal Hill are more convoluted and can be traced back to Standard Oil of California. Texaco originally started as a company purchasing crude oil after the 1901 Spindletop discovery in East Texas. By 1908, they were drilling wells and refining. By 1928, Texaco operated over 4,000 gas stations in all forty-eight states. Texaco and Standard Oil of California formed a joint venture in 1936—Caltex. Texaco was also impacted by the Arab oil embargo and the emerging nationalism movement in the Middle East. In 1972, Saudi Arabia nationalized Aramco, in which Texaco had a 50% ownership interest. Libya nationalized Texaco Overseas Petroleum Company, which was owned by Texaco, in 1979. By the end of the decade, Caltex was nationalized by Iran in the Islamic Revolution. Texaco began an effort to withdraw from unprofitable markets and oil fields. It was estimated that Texaco's net profits dropped from $1.6 billion to $830.6 million at the start of the Arab oil embargo and remained at this level throughout the 1970s. Texaco faced additional financial pressures in the early 1990s, laying off 2,000 employees in 1993. They would be gone from Signal Hill by 1994.

Exxon traces its lineage back to its purchase of Humble Oil, which in turn purchased the remaining gas stations from Signal Oil in 1967. Like the Shell Oil Company, Exxon was impacted by the Arab oil embargo and began to expand their operations in the North Sea, the Gulf of Mexico, Africa, and Asia. Exxon faced its own environmental disaster when the *Exxon Valdez* oil tanker struck Bligh Reef in Prince William Sound in Alaska on March 24, 1989. Over eleven million gallons of crude oil were spilled, resulting in a massive loss of aquatic life and seabirds, as well as an impact on the fishing industry that resulted in years of cleanup efforts and litigation. Congress passed the Oil Pollution Act of 1990 in a direct response to the spill. Nine years later, Exxon would be completely out of Signal Hill. Signal Hill Petroleum purchased the working interest in the Signal Hill West Unit from Exxon in 1999. In the same year, they also purchased the royalty interest in a number of East Unit properties from the Alamitos Land Company to complete the development of the Bixby Ridge subdivision and the construction of Discovery Well Park.

Oil Is Discovered! Again.

The US Geological Survey has made various surveys over the decades to attempt to determine the amount of oil and gas still locked in the strata underneath Signal Hill. These estimates have ranged from a few hundred thousand barrels to two billion barrels. Using the latest technology, in 2012, Signal Hill Petroleum (who operates the oil field units) conducted an extensive survey for new oil and gas deposits in the Long Beach Field.

Traditional oil field reserve surveys include exploding charges of dynamite below the surface to create seismic waves that reflect off the strata. These seismic waves are then recorded and mapped. The use of explosives, however, is out of the question in heavily developed urban areas. The Signal Hill Petroleum survey involved the use of seismic monitoring equipment, which was arrayed throughout the area in a grid pattern, and the use of special vibration trucks. The trucks deployed metal pads directly onto the streets, and these plates were then vibrated between low and high frequencies. The seismic waves then bounced off of the strata and this data was collected by hundreds of the monitoring devices. With the use of supercomputing, a three-dimensional model of the oil fields below Signal Hill was developed. The model revealed that major pockets of oil and gas still exist—pockets that can be reached by new drilling techniques.

The seismic survey was a paradigm shift: Prior to this time, urban planners believed that the oil field would be played out by the 1990s. Earlier wells has been drilled to depths of 4,000 to 5,000 feet. By the summer of 2015, Signal Hill Petroleum was drilling to depths of 10,000 feet. The seismic survey also showed that significant oil and gas deposits are found on both sides of the Newport–Inglewood Fault. The Los Angeles region may in fact be sitting atop the largest combined urban oil reserves in the world. Signal Hill Petroleum is not sharing their estimates of how much oil and gas is locked below the surface, but at the current rate of one million barrels a year being

After years of aggressive oil drilling, extensive soil decontamination was required before the land could be redeveloped. The contaminated soil was a distinct green.

Reclamation efforts continue. The man in the middle of this photograph is inspecting an old oil well casing.

pumped from below Signal Hill, it appears the field could be producing for centuries.

There has always been a dynamic tension between the City and Signal Hill Petroleum, which is interested in preserving access to the oil field, while the City is interested in furthering the economic development of the community. This tension is likely to persist as the community continues to reclaim itself and as oil production keeps generating revenues.[2]

The Town without a "Downtown"

Today it is difficult to visualize the uncertainties faced by Signal Hill in the 1970s. Signal Hill had been left out of the economic prosperity that came from GIs returning home from World War II, marrying, starting families, and purchasing homes. What vacant land existed was hopelessly contaminated by prior oil field uses and was encumbered by oil leases. The multistory, high density residential development of the 1962 General Plan was turning out to be a mirage. The community lacked a downtown with basic retail businesses and services for the residents. The City had been split into north and south sections by the construction of the San Diego Freeway in 1965. Pacific Coast Highway, Redondo Avenue, Cherry Avenue, and Willow Street were dotted with used-car lots, junkyards, and dilapidated oil field businesses.

In the formative years, the SHRDA financed infrastructure improvements necessary to support the rebirth of the community. Like most redevelopment agencies in their early years, the SHRDA needed advance funds to begin operations. The then-sizable amount of $7.5 million was advanced from the City in 1977. Documents from this time stated that the Los Angeles County Tax Assessor was anticipating a decline in oil reserves at 15% per year until the reserves were depleted. Budget documents indicate that the SHRDA was involved in the rehabilitation of the library on Hill Street and the remodeling of the police station, also on Hill Street. The SHRDA began waterline installation and street widening on Cherry Avenue, the City's main north–south artery; redevelopment of Cherry Avenue with new commercial enterprises; a façade improvement program on Cherry Avenue for businesses impacted by the street widening; the construction of sewers on Obispo Avenue; street improvements on Walnut, 25th Street, Junipero Avenue, and Combellack Drive; and the acquisition of the land for what would become Hillbrook Park. By December 1985, the SHRDA's property tax increment revenues had sufficiently grown to support a $28 million bond issue.

The SHRDA also participated in a multiyear project of widening Spring Street, starting from the eastern City limits with Long Beach and, over the decades, completing the widening to Long Beach Boulevard. The City and SHRDA accepted that the agency eventually had to take the lead in constructing the major infrastructure projects needed by the City as well as the region, which meant managing the Spring Street project, even in the City of Long Beach area. The City and SHRDA also recognized the regional importance of the widening of the intersection of Cherry Avenue and Pacific Coast Highway to relieve traffic congestion, and they took the lead on the construction of the intersection project even though it was located entirely in Long Beach. Otherwise the project might never have been done. These major street and utility projects were not constructed in a vacuum: the City was beginning to implement a vision for the new community.

We will never know if early developers G. W. Hughes and Joe Denni envisioned a downtown for Signal Hill. There is evidence that scattered stores started to appear on Cherry Avenue, north of State Street (Pacific Coast Highway) in the late 1890s. On the west side of Cherry Avenue at 29th Street sat the T-Bone Good Eats Inn and the Chas W. Woods tools and supplies store. The Hinshaw Building on Cherry Avenue and 21st Street had a small convenience grocery store. However, the discovery of oil on June 23, 1921, and the attendant rush to develop oil would, for some time, prevent any chance that Signal Hill would have a downtown.

From the 1930s through the 1950s, there were scattered commercial establishments constructed to serve the needs of the oil-field workers—like Kid Mexico's "Miracle Block," located on Orange Street just above Hill Street. Todd "Kid Mexico" Faulkner was born in 1900 and was a well-known prize fighter. He started his boxing career in Taft, California, at the age of ten, and won the state bantamweight crown in 1914, the welterweight crown in 1917, and the middleweight crown in 1925. By the 1920s, he was promoting fights at his ring in Huntington Beach. His Miracle Block on Orange Avenue contained an eight-lane bowling alley, a cocktail lounge, and a restaurant, as well as a large auditorium, where oil-field workers and their families were entertained by famous celebrities, including Hopalong Cassidy and Jack Dempsey.

Faulkner was the closest thing Signal Hill had to a political boss. He operated an illegal bingo parlor, and for a while the Signal Hill Police Department looked the other way. Each year, he held a giant Christmas Party for the youth in Signal Hill and reportedly gave away thousands of toys. Faulkner was convicted of election fraud when he attempted to register non–Signal Hill residents to vote in

This postcard featured Kid Mexico's Miracle Block and advertised the new bowling lanes, an elaborate auditorium, and dining and dancing in the "Signal" room. The postcard also mentioned that "Everyone enjoys Games of Skill." One of his games resulted in Kid Mexico being arrested and found guilty of running an illegal gaming operation, c. 1940s. (Courtesy of City of Signal Hill.)

Kid Mexico ingratiated himself to the community by holding large Christmas parties where gifts were given away to the children, c. 1940s. (Courtesy of City of Signal Hill.)

the 1952 municipal election where an anti-bingo ordinance was on the ballot. It passed. Without bingo, his business slowly declined.

Discouraged with Signal Hill, Faulkner moved to Laguna Beach, where off-duty Signal Hill Police officers helped him build a new road to his home. Soon after locating to Laguna Beach, Faulkner had federal tax liens placed on his properties for failure to pay $267,000 in back taxes. He was broke and eventually returned to his home in Signal Hill at 2332 Cerritos Avenue, where he established the Kid Mexico Museum. He advertised the museum as better than Knott's Berry Farm and Disneyland combined. Faulkner died on September 6, 1986, and was buried in Sunnyside Cemetery in Long Beach.[3]

There was no shortage of unique restaurants and lounges in Signal Hill. The Denni carriage house was moved across Skyline Drive

Near the center of this photograph, surrounded by palm trees, is the Denni mansion, and just to its left is the Palla mansion. These, and other grand residences, were built prior to the discovery of oil, when Signal Hill was a lovely little town near the coast. By 1940, when this photo was taken, the Dennis, Pallas, and anyone else with money had long since moved from the industrial cacophony of the Hill. The Denni carriage house got a second life when it relocated a block away on Skyline Drive, where it became the Hilltop Restaurant, bottom center, in this photograph. (Courtesy of City of Signal Hill.)

by Richmond Oil Company and was converted into the Hilltop Star Room Restaurant. Considered upscale, with live music and a dance floor, the Star Room is fondly remembered by locals for its views of Long Beach. The restaurant eventually closed and was demolished. The location is currently Sunset View Park, and debris from the former carriage house was found in the ravine below the park.[4]

For over fifty years, Bonnie Price operated the Foothill Club, located on Cherry Avenue and 19th Street. She had the distinction of being the first woman in California to hold a liquor license in her own name. In 1936, Price converted the building to the famous club, hosting country music greats like Johnny Cash, George Jones, Merle Haggard and the Collins Kids. The Foothill Club was a favorite hangout for the sailors and marines stationed at the Long Beach Naval Base, so much so that a taxi stand was set up outside the nightclub. Unchanged since 1937, the retro club was the location of the bar scene in the 2000 film *Nurse Betty* staring Chris Rock and Renee Zellweger. Price passed away in 2008, and the club was eventually demolished, becoming the site of new residences.[5]

Prior to the construction of the San Diego Freeway through Signal Hill and Long Beach in 1965, Pacific Coast Highway served as the east–west highway in the region. As with many highways of this era, strip commercial development abounded for the highway's entire length through Signal Hill. An assortment of used car lots, motels, fast food restaurants, auto repair shops and other auto-oriented businesses lined the highway. The growing residential community was vocal in its requests that development offer commercial and service uses that were found in the surrounding communities.

After the formation of the SHRDA, industrial developers began to see the potential of building planned industrial business parks in the community. The area east of Cherry Avenue and north of Willow Street began to develop with several such business parks. Eastman Office Products constructed a warehouse on the north side of Willow Street, just east of Cherry Avenue for their growing office supplies and furniture business. In 1986, Eastman moved, entering a fifteen-year lease for a 460,000-square-foot distribution facility on a twelve-acre parcel in the Long Beach–Signal Hill Business Center at

This early photograph shows Eastman's Business Interior Showroom on Willow Street. By 1986, they had grown so large that they needed to move to a new facility. (Courtesy of City of Signal Hill.)

Office Depot, c. 2000. It became one of the City's largest sales-tax revenue generators. (Courtesy of City of Signal Hill.)

Willow Street and Redondo Avenue. A second phase for Eastman's distribution activities would involve the demolition of the former Long Beach General Hospital, located on the east side of Redondo Avenue, to allow for expansion. By 1993, the Eastman facility would be purchased by Office Depot and used as their main distribution facility for office supplies and office furniture for most of Southern California. The importance of this business to the region was underscored by Signal Hill and Long Beach together forming the Spring Street Corridor Joint Powers Authority, a planning authority that

The Long Beach–Signal Hill Business Center broke ground on March 2, 1986. Second from the right is Signal Hill Mayor Louie Dare, and to his immediate left is Los Angeles County Supervisor Dean Dana. The $50-million business center was the site of a former County hospital. It was demolished to make way for the Eastman Building, which was developed by Goldrich & Kest. Los Angeles County leased the land for the twenty-six-acre business park as part of their economic development efforts. (Courtesy of City of Signal Hill.)

entered into joint agreements to assist the business succeed. Office Depot grew to be one of the City's single, largest sales-tax producers, which helped stabilize the community's budget.[6]

Industrial development may have continued along the Willow Street corridor and perhaps there would be no Town Center today, except for the approval of the Willow Ridge condominium development. Due in part to the insatiable need for additional residential development in many parts of Southern California, developers converted industrial- and commercial-zoned areas for the construction of residences. Willow Ridge was Signal Hill's first true large-scale, planned residential development and was a major gamble at the time due to its location in the oil field. The 160-unit phased development began construction in 1980 and was completed in 1984. The development included gated access with a twenty-four-hour manned gatehouse, a large clubhouse, a pool, and other features, which demonstrated that people would live in the former oil field with the proper development standards and amenities. The character of the community would change as more planned residential development would follow upon the success of Willow Ridge.

The Father of the Superstore Comes to Town

Due in part to the influx of new residents, the City's 1986 comprehensive general plan envisioned that the intersection of Cherry Avenue and Willow Street would be the future town center for the community. Though it was hoped that retail uses could be drawn to the area, the distance from the San Diego Freeway (I-405) made this unlikely without SHRDA intervention. The general plan envisioned Town Center East, Town Center West, Town Center North, and the Commercial Corridor Specific Plan. The general plan was later amended in 2001 to include the Heritage Square Central Business District, which became a mixed-use commercial/residential neighborhood immediately adjacent to the Town Center West project. A major complaint from residents in preparing the general plan was that community members needed to travel outside for even the basic necessities—for example, there was no grocery store in the growing community.

Willow Ridge condominium development was so successful that residential developers wanted to continue condominium and townhome development along the Willow Street corridor, since developers argued that retail development would never locate in the town center area. This prediction might have proven true, except for the intervention of a remarkable visionary. Born in 1916, Sol Price was the son of Russian immigrants. (He was no relation to Bonnie Price who operated Signal Hill's Foothill Club for decades, starting in the 1930s.) Price pioneered his commercial development model with FedMart in 1954 and then Price Club in 1976. Price was practicing law in San Diego when friends convinced him to look at the Los Angeles area for new superstores.

In order to keep overhead low, Price would locate his stores on cheaper industrial land, instead of locating in shopping malls or along major highways. He started FedMart in a rundown warehouse near the Port of San Diego. The retail warehouse chain eventually grew to forty-one stores. In 1976, Price was forced out of FedMart by his German partners. Within months, he and his son opened Price Club in an old airplane hangar in San Diego once used by Howard Hughes. Price charged $25 for an annual membership for the warehouse store, where you could find supersized boxes and jars of your favorite household foods and goods. At its zenith in 1992, there were ninety-four Price Clubs in the United States, Canada, and Mexico, earning $134 million in profits on $6.6 billion in sales. By 1993, Price Club had merged with Costco.[7]

As the City was in desperate need for sales tax revenues, in 1985 the SHRDA and Price teamed up to bring a Price Club to Signal Hill. Price liked the rundown portion of the oil field located at the intersection of Cherry Avenue and Willow Street—Town Center East. The property contained numerous oil wells and over 2,400 absentee owners as a direct result of the unregulated oil speculation from the 1920s. The project would need SHRDA assistance to work: eminent domain to assemble the numerous ownerships, working with Signal Hill Petroleum on abandoning selected wells and leaving some wells in production, and construction of a large retaining wall to hold back the hill. Price imposed a strict deadline on the SHRDA to make the deal happen, or he was moving on. The development was not without its dissenters, especially from the newly adjacent residents of Willow Ridge.

As the City and the SHRDA began to consider the development, over 140 Willow Ridge residents signed a petition opposed to the new warehouse store. They were concerned about traffic, noise, and crime, among other things. The petition eventually grew to 275 individuals, as residents throughout Signal Hill opposed the new warehouse store. In light of the total number of Signal Hill registered voters, this was an extremely large number. Working to mitigate objectionable aspects of the project and unfazed by the opponents, the city council and the SHRDA approved plans for the 114,400-square-foot warehouse store in 1986.

Approval of the Price Club hinged on the vote of an unlikely person, Louis "Louie" Dare, who had become mayor during the Price Club controversies. Dare was born in 1919 and grew up in Pennsylvania.

During the depths of the Great Depression, Dare joined the Civilian Conservation Corp, working in Wyoming. He moved to West Virginia, where he worked at steel mill and machine shop. Later he would work as a machinist for the Goodyear Tire Company and enlisted in the Army Air Corp in World War II where he learned to fly planes and worked as an airplane mechanic. He moved to Signal Hill in 1953 and started Quality Tool and Die on Ohio Avenue. The hilltop still was bristling with oil wells and tanks when Dare moved in.

Dare was known as a staunch fiscal conservative. Opposed to government intervention in business, he initially did not support the use of eminent domain to assist the Price Club in any way. However, he came to see the project's value to the redevelopment of Signal Hill, and he certainly recognized the need for sales tax revenues to fund municipal services. The city attorney at the time, Dave Aleshire, persuaded Mayor Dare to join the other council members and support use of the redevelopment agency to deal with the environmental issues from the oil field uses as well as to encourage economic development and the generation of sales taxes as a replacement revenue for declining oil revenues. During his time in office, Dare would also be involved in the development of Eastman Office Products, the Signal Hill Auto Mall, and California Crown planned housing project.

In 1985–1986, Dare needed to lead the City during contentious times with the Price Club development. Lead he did, despite withering attacks from Willow Ridge residents. The Price Club was approved and showed that Signal Hill could support retail development that wasn't located adjacent to the freeway or on a major highway. There were threats of council recalls and Dare would lose his seat on the city council during the next election in two years. Longtime–council member Mike Noll commented that Dare was a pioneer who, although he lost his seat, would eventually return to the council to do many good things for the community.

City Attorney Dave Aleshire compared Dare's support of the Price Club to the acts of bravery presented in President Kennedy's book *Profiles in Courage.* Dare knew he would lose the Willow Ridge voters, and the Price Club vote would cost him his seat on the council. However, he went ahead, against his concerns over eminent domain

The success of the Price Club in Signal Hill demonstrated that retail uses could locate in the former oil field area, and it kicked off a series of retail developments in the budding Town Center at the intersection of Cherry Avenue and Willow Street, c. 1990s. (Courtesy of City of Signal Hill.)

and his conservative values, to approve the first major commercial development in Signal Hill. Aleshire suggested that perhaps all the future commercial success that Signal Hill experienced flowed from this one decision. It is easy in hindsight to see how courageous and important his decision was.[8]

The Price Club would go on to anchor the twenty-four-acre Town Center East project. Subsequently, the Home Depot and PetSmart were drawn to the site along with restaurants, coffee shops, a bank, and other retailers and service uses. This was one of the first retail developments that involved the participation of Signal Hill Petroleum in working with the City to abandon oil wells and integrate active oil wells within the parking lot, with low-profile pumping units. At one point, not being able to find space in Town Center East, Toys "R" Us developed a stand-alone site north on Cherry Avenue that eventually became the Best Buy. The second major retail development was the OfficeMax, Del Taco, and Togo's, which developed under the Commercial Corridor Specific Plan in 1999. This became known as Town Center North. This development leapfrogged older development on Cherry Avenue.

A few remaining oil wells overlook the Town Center East development.

With the Town Center East fully developed, a new commercial center, called Town Center West, developed on the south side of Willow Street in 2003. Here, a Food 4 Less (the City's first grocery store), Coco's (now a Black Bear Diner), Starbucks (the City's first), Chevron, McDonald's and other retail shops and restaurants developed. The fourth development in the Town Center area is the Heritage Square Central Business District and was amended into the 2001 General Plan. The SHRDA assisted with the development of a Fresh & Easy Market (now Mother's Market), which opened in September 2010. These new developments required active intervention by the SHRDA to assist developers in well closures, soil cleanup, and infrastructure improvements, and they included working with Signal Hill Petroleum.

The 2001 General Plan anticipated additional demand for retail commercial development on the Cherry/Willow corridor. Eventually, commercial uses would begin to locate adjacent to the San Diego Freeway. The investment of the SHRDA in the Spring Street widening, from the Auto Center to Atlantic Avenue, as well as the installation of sewers by the SHRDA, allowed the Gateway Center to develop in 2012—at the intersection of Spring Street and Atlantic Avenue, at the I-405 Freeway. By this time, Signal Hill had two Home Depots, two Starbucks, and dozens of retail and service uses for the community. This was quite the accomplishment for a city that was told by many a developer that retail uses would never locate in the former oil field.

Oil and McDonald's in the Town Center West development.

An active well (left) sits in the midst of a parking lot in the Gateway development.

The past and the future are on display at Mother's Market, 2019. Mounted on this exterior wall of the grocery store is a historic photo of the oil field. Adjacent to the historic photo are charging stations for electric vehicles like the one pictured here.

, Costco is one of the City's largest individual sales tax producers, and the other retailers generate significant revenues for community services. Economic development attracting retail uses was only
one goal of the SHRDA. By the 1990s, the community was actively
courting auto dealers who needed to relocate out of Long Beach in
order to survive.

It's Not Easy to Escape Your Past: The Signal Hill Auto Center

Just as Signal Hill's early development was altered by the construction of the Pacific Electric Railway line from downtown Los Angeles
to Long Beach in 1902, the construction of a second mass transit line
would alter Signal Hill eighty years later. With the rapid growth of
automobile ownership in the 1920s, the region faced growing traffic congestion. By 1937, the Automobile Club of Southern California
suggested a network of parkways—restricted-access motorways to
speed along vehicles.

An Auto Club survey that year illustrated that the streetcars were
averaging speeds of from eleven to fifteen miles per hour within ten
miles of downtown Los Angeles, and that vehicle–streetcar collisions
were on the rise. After World War II, the Pacific Electric Railway was
slowly being viewed by the public as substandard compared to owning one's own car—the personal vehicle was the wave of the future.
The extensive passenger rail system was slowly phased out and dismantled. Ironically, the system's last Red Car run, in 1961, was from
Los Angeles to Long Beach; the system's first Red Car had traveled
the same route fifty-nine years earlier, in 1902.

With the success of the Arroyo Parkway (later renamed the Pasadena Freeway), which opened in December 1940, the next forty
years were consumed with building the regional freeway system as
the solution to growing traffic congestion. However, by the 1970s,
traffic congestion continued to worsen even with the new freeways.
The Los Angeles County Transportation Commission (LACTC) was
formed in 1976 to resurrect mass transit as a solution to the region's
gridlock. In a "history repeats itself" moment, the LACTC proposed that its first light rail line be constructed from downtown Los
Angeles to downtown Long Beach. The new light rail line became

a reality when the voters in Los Angeles County approved a half-cent (.5%) sales tax increase in 1980 to be used for mass transit projects. Three additional half-cent sales tax increases for mass transit would be approved over the next three decades.

However, there was a significant difference between the new Long Beach Blue Line alignment and the former Red Car alignment. Transit planners wanted to make a direct connection to downtown Long Beach. The route selected by the planners traveled in the street medians on Long Beach Boulevard, south of the San Diego Freeway and through Long Beach. This route alignment decision would create great consequences, which would play out over the subsequent decades. The groundbreaking for the Blue Line light rail line was on October 31, 1990, and the line opened on March 1, 1995. It soon became the nation's busiest light rail line in passenger ridership.[9]

The economic prosperity in the post–World War II era saw Long Beach Boulevard become the region's "auto row," with numerous makes and models available. In 1955, Mike Salta opened his first dealership on Long Beach Boulevard—Master's Pontiac. It would grow to become the largest Pontiac dealership in the nation. By the 1980s, Long Beach Boulevard's auto row consisted of Long Beach Honda, Long Beach BMW and Mazda, Long Beach Nissan, and other dealers. The dealerships were opposed to the new Blue Line alignment, since it caused vehicular circulation and access issues for them. After failing to resolve these issues and then failing to find a suitable new location in Long Beach, the dealers were ready to relocate.

Just as the Lakewood Mall initiated the era of shopping malls—wreaking havoc on traditional strip commercial corridors—the concept of the "auto mall" would kick off a sea change for auto rows. Barely a few miles north of Signal Hill, in 1979, the City of Cerritos began work on the Cerritos Auto Center, later known as the Cerritos Auto Square. The auto mall began with the purchase of 8.5 acres at Studebaker and 183rd Street. The Cerritos Redevelopment Agency worked with the dealerships to design road improvements, landscaped medians and parkways, waterfalls and decorative streetlights, along with New Orleans themed building architecture. Chevrolet became the first dealership, opening in 1980. The auto mall would grow to become—at one point—the world's largest auto mall, with twenty-three brands and over 10,000 vehicles in inventory on any day. Perhaps most noteworthy, the auto mall became the City's largest sales tax revenue source. As the auto mall was being developed, Dave Aleshire was the deputy city attorney for the City of Cerritos. Good fortune favored the City of Signal Hill. When Aleshire moved on, he landed in the City and became Signal Hill's long-time city attorney. The City benefited greatly from what he had learned from development of the Cerritos auto mall.[10]

The Long Beach dealers began a dialogue with the SHRDA, which resulted in the City of Signal Hill approving a thirty-five-acre Signal Hill Auto Center at the intersection of Cherry Avenue and Spring Street. This was in 1989, through the Auto Center Specific Plan. Not surprisingly, challenges for development of the Auto Center included severe soil contamination, improperly abandoned oil wells, leaking pipelines, fractured ownership and lot patterns, lack of adequate streets, and undersized water lines and sewers. The first development agreement was reached between Bob Autry of Long Beach BMW/Mazda and the SHRDA. Soon, other dealers followed Autry's lead and entered into development agreements, including Mike Salta, Glenn Thomas Dodge, Long Beach Nissan, and Long Beach Honda. A major part of the Auto Center ended up on land owned by the Robinette family. It had been the site of a turkey farm in the 1910s and then later, a site for oil related uses. The Robinettes were opposed to the use of eminent domain; however, after a good deal of negotiations they agreed to long-term leases that would make the investments by the dealers economical and grant bank loan approvals.

During the early grading for the Signal Hill Auto Center, City contractors uncovered thousands of tons of contaminated soil. The original estimate for the cleanup cost was $1.1 million for three dealerships, but it ballooned rapidly to $6.1 million for just these three, located on Cherry Avenue between Spring Street and 29th Street. Mayor Louie Dare commented that the City never thought it would

"Working together for a Better Community." Louie Dare was returned by the voters to the city council after he lost his seat due to his support of the Price Club. Dare was instrumental in planning and approvals for the Signal Hill Auto Center in the 1990s. Pictured here is the Signal Hill Redevelopment Agency's project sign for the Glenn E. Thomas Dodge dealership, c. 1992. The dealership moved from Long Beach to its new home in Signal Hill. (Courtesy of City of Signal Hill.)

run into as much contamination as it had on Cherry Avenue. However, Dare continued to support the project. In the end, 36,000 tons of contaminated soil were trucked away to be remediated. When studies determined that the cleanup would cost over $120 million, and soil would need to be excavated to one hundred feet below the surface, the SHRDA eventually worked with the State to install a vapor recovery system to mitigate the costs of cleanup. The community was painfully discovering that it was not easy to escape its oil-field past.

There were other significant improvements to make the Auto Center successful, including the construction of the Auto Center freeway sign in 1994 and an addition of 13.74 acres to the Auto Center in 2009. The latter was a risky move, since the country was in the grips of the Great Recession—the period of general economic decline during the late 2000s and early 2010s. There were major restructurings of the "Big Three" auto manufacturers underway, as General

The Signal Hill Redevelopment Agency reached its first Auto Center agreement with Long Beach BMW, shown here c. early 2000s. They chose, under the "first dealership to come—first dealership to choose their site" policy, to locate at the intersection of Cherry Avenue and Spring Street, the most prominent corner of the Signal Hill Auto Center. (Courtesy of City of Signal Hill.)

Unlike some of the other auto centers, Signal Hill's Auto Center lacks direct visibility from the I-405 Freeway.The auto dealers' association and the City worked with Caltrans to permit the construction of an Auto Center freeway sign. The original sign was constructed in 1994 on leased property, which the SHRDA eventually purchased. The sign was upgraded in 2018 (as shown here) through the participation of the City and the dealers. (Courtesy of City of Signal Hill.)

Motors and Chrysler accepted federal financial help in order to survive. Over 2,000 dealerships were forced to close nationwide as the manufacturers terminated dealership franchise agreements. Only the strong dealers would survive the Recession's impacts. By 2009, Palmer Mercedes Benz in Long Beach was purchased by Damien Shelly and moved into the Auto Center. Long Beach Coast Cadillac was purchased by Brad Willingham and Ron Charone in 2012; they remodeled the former Pontiac store for the relocated dealership.

Over a period of several years, the SHRDA also purchased the GATX tank farm and relocated A&A Concrete from the Auto Center. The US EPA was instrumental in using the Superfund to clean up a former small refinery that had been converted to a waste-oil processing facility and shuttered by its operators, leaving hundreds of drums of waste oil on the site. Once the site was assembled and remediated, CarMax began planning a dealership on the location. However, the Great Recession derailed the project. The site eventually was purchased by Sonic Motors for the relocation of the Long Beach BMW store. MINI Cooper then remodeled the former BMW store. The Signal Hill Auto Center continues to provide significant sales tax revenues to fund City services.[11]

"We Love What Seems to Be Impossible": Signal Hill Gets a New Police Station

Saturday January 26, 2013, was a cloudy day as Signal Hill Mayor Tina Hansen presided over the ceremonies opening the new Signal Hill Police Station to the community. She reflected that one of the first actions of the original city council was to form its own police department. This meant breaking away from the Los Angeles County Sheriff's Department, which had patrolled the area prior to incorporation of the City. In 1924, the police station was housed in temporary buildings on Cherry Avenue and remained there until it moved into the new combined police and fire station on Hill Street in 1931. The police department outgrew the Hill Street facility, which was then remodeled in the 1970s to accommodate the department. By the 1990s, it was recognized that the City needed to either add on to the existing station or construct a new police station, as every

When the City incorporated in 1924, it formed its own municipal fire department. The City's station was first located on the east side of Cherry Avenue at 19th Street and would later be demolished for the Foothill Club. The department purchased its 1924 American La France fire engine from the Los Angeles County Fire Department. The fire engine is currently part of the collection of the Los Angeles County Fire Department Museum in the City of Bellflower. (Courtesy of City of Signal Hill.)

In the early 1930s, the fire department moved to the City's Hill Street facility, shown above. The City joined the Los Angeles County Fire Protection District in 1968, and in 1978 the department moved to their new station, Station 60, which is located at 2300 East 27th Street. (Courtesy of City of Signal Hill.)

The police station and fire station on Hill Street, just west of the City Hall, 1965. These buildings would be modified in the late 1970s by the SHRDA. It wasn't until 2013 that the police department had a new station. (Courtesy of City of Signal Hill.)

available space was being used, including converting a closet into an office for the sergeant.

In due course, the city council formed a citizen's committee to weigh the option of remodeling the existing station or building a new one. The committee recommended a new station, as the existing station did not meet public safety building standards and would require extensive remodeling in addition to expansion. However, there were financial hurdles: the City could not afford a bond issue to construct the new station and also purchase the land needed. The citizen committee recommended that the council place on the ballot a 3% utility tax to fund a bond issue. The utility tax ballot question became Proposition H, and it was scheduled for the California special election in 2005.

In hindsight, the timing of this decision proved to be fateful, since Governor Arnold Schwarzenegger proposed four constitutional amendments for the state's special election. The amendments attacked teacher tenure, prohibited the use of union dues for political purposes, created state budget limitations, and changed the redistricting process. This statewide election would become the most expensive election in state history, as the California Teachers Association spent $56 million to defeat the tenure measure; they

The newly constructed Signal Hill police station opened in February 2013. (Courtesy of City of Signal Hill.)

even mortgaged their headquarters building in Sacramento to raise campaign funds. All of Governor Schwarzenegger's measures were defeated. Angry voters carried their "no" votes on to the police station tax measure. The voters spoke, and the City of Signal Hill went back to the drawing board.[12]

The City explored eighteen station locations as part of the revised planning process and landed on a three-acre parcel, owned by the SHRDA, at the west end of the Auto Center. It was felt that the City needed to save the costs of purchasing land by using the SHRDA's parcel, which was allowed under the redevelopment plan. The station planning process had moved far down the road by 2007; however, the city attorney felt that the City should explore a vacant, four-acre parcel of land that was still heavily encumbered by oil leases dating back from the 1920s, as a result of lingering oil speculation in the community. The SHRDA then moved to purchase the land and to construct the Signal Hill police station. This $18 million project included the purchase of over 5,500 ownership interests in the four-acre parcel of land. SHRDA records showed that between 1922 and 1931 the parcel had been divided into 7,000 oil shares.

It required three years for the city attorney to track down as many owners as possible and to complete the condemnation action on over 1,500 owners of interests who could not be located. The deeds that their grandparents had purchased in the 1920s had long ago disappeared. The SHRDA then issued a bond to construct the facility. The new 21,500-square-foot station eclipsed the existing 13,000-square-foot Hill Street station, and the property was large enough to accommodate the new station and include land for future building expansion. As Mayor Hansen presided over the ribbon cutting for the station, she declared "We love what seems to be impossible," and stated that Signal Hill was a city with vision, and that it might take time to figure out how to reach its goals, but that the City is patient. That patience would be sorely tested with the SHRDA's final public project—the new Signal Hill Library.[13]

Signal Hill Gets Its Own Library

Prior the twentieth century, libraries were viewed as a place only for scholars and the elite. Up until the 1890s, the few public libraries had membership fees. It was not until Andrew Carnegie, the steel and railroad baron, began his nationwide library-building project in 1890 that communities began to see public libraries as an asset. Carnegie was decidedly motivated to build free public libraries. One reason was that he was so poor as a child in his native Scotland that he could not afford the two-dollar fee to use the local library. Carnegie also believed that in order to survive, democracies needed an educated electorate. Of course, one pathway to being educated was to be well-read.

Carnegie was also of the opinion that we are born with nothing and that one should die with nothing. When Carnegie reached middle age, he devoted the rest of his life to giving away his fortune. The Carnegie Library grants funded close to 1,700 public libraries throughout the nation, in 1,400 cities. Cities lobbied for the grants and committed to supporting the operation of their libraries with tax funds and to never charging a membership fee. Signal Hill's incorporating in 1924 was too late to apply for a Carnegie grant. However, public libraries were important to the new city council and the community: one of the first actions taken by the city council was to break from the county library system and form the City's own municipal library. Jessie Nelson, as mayor and also a newspaper reporter, recognized the importance of reading and advocated for the library.[14]

Signal Hill's first library was housed in a temporary building at 2120 Cherry Avenue. Mary Trood, appointed by the city council in 1924, was the first librarian. The library reported in 1925 that 1,600 books were loaned out, and by 1930, the collection had grown to over 3,000 books. Upon completion of the new city hall in 1934, the library moved into the upstairs of the building and quickly ran out of space. It was then moved to the downstairs floor of city hall, where it was known as the "cellar library." At 800 square feet, it had the unique distinction of being the smallest library in the country at the time. It was from this location that librarian Trood retired in 1965, after serving the City for close to forty years.

The next move would be into the vacant engine house of the Signal Hill Fire Department, when the county fire staff moved out and into the newly constructed fire station in the 1970s. The new library

After being housed in a temporary building, the City's library, shown here in the 1930s, was located in the upper floor of city hall. It was relocated to the basement of city hall in the 1960s, where it was known as the "cellar library" by local wags. Outgrowing the 800-square-foot basement space, in the late 1970s it moved to the vacated engine house of the former fire station. (Courtesy of City of Signal Hill.)

was a "spacious" 4,234 square feet. Each time the library moved it was due to space considerations, but technology started to play a role in later years. For example, the former engine house was not only too small for the growing community, but its technology was outdated.[15]

The City began planning for a new library in 2000, with its destiny tied to new revenue from the SHRDA. Through a series of fits and starts—including issuing a redevelopment bond to construct the new library and the very real threatened takeaway of the bond proceeds from the state—for years, the new library was never a sure thing. A new library was the dream of Tina Hansen, long-term mayor and council member, and despite uncertainties, she pressed on. In particular, she took a hands-on approach to designing the library, ensuring that the library reflected the community's history.[16]

The State Shutters Redevelopment Agencies Statewide— Signal Hill Fights for a New Library

Governor Jerry Brown held several elected offices—including sixteen years serving as governor in the 1970s and then again in the 2010s. He also served as Oakland's mayor from 1999 to 2007. When Brown was elected to his third term as governor in 2010, California city officials could have assumed that he understood the important role that redevelopment agencies played in the rebuilding of their blighted communities. For that term, California was in the grips of the Great Recession. The State faced a $28 billion shortfall in its budget. Governor Brown's 2011 budget message proposed closing some of this gap by dissolving all of the redevelopment agencies statewide. He hoped that such action would free up $5.5 billion in redevelopment agency property tax revenues to be diverted to the public schools, which by law required State funding. Brown termed redevelopment agencies "futile" and a "zero sum game." Critics of redevelopment pounced, and conveniently forgotten in the debate were the well-managed redevelopment agencies, like Signal Hill's, that were pulling their communities out of blight and not abusing redevelopment's powers.[17]

The shuttering of the SHRDA by the State of California in 2011 delivered a serious blow to the community. At that time, several

The Signal Hill Redevelopment Agency was instrumental in providing the funding for the new Signal Hill Library. The new library would be the last capital improvement by the SHRDA. It capped off an investment of over $102.2 million by the Agency in environmental cleanup, infrastructure construction, and capital projects that significantly improved the quality of life in Signal Hill.

important projects were underway, including the new police station and the detailed planning of the Signal Hill Library. Both were placed into jeopardy by the dissolution. The SHRDA had issued a bond to fund the construction of the new library, and the bond was at risk. Critics wanted the city council to give up on the new library; they did not see any value to its construction.

Council Member Hansen asserted that the City would fight tooth and nail for the $8.6 million bond for the library. "I know that there are people who think we should not build this library," Hansen said, "and I know there are people who think libraries are obsolete. All I know is that anytime I go to any kind of family event at the library, it's bursting at the seams." Council Member Edward Wilson agreed by stating, "What we're talking about is continuing to invest in the City or to have the money go someplace else . . . I, for one, would rather see the money in Signal Hill."

After several years of work in Sacramento, including legislation, the City was able to salvage the bond funding for the new library. It would be more than triple the size of the old one: from a 4,234-square-foot library housed in the former Signal Hill fire engine house to a 14,000-square-foot, two-story building. The new library opened in the summer of 2019 and has over 30,000 books in its collection. Also, through cooperative agreements with other libraries, there are literally hundreds of thousands of books available to its patrons. Besides stacks of books and audio/visual media, the first floor is home to a community room, reading areas, a learning center, a history room, and study rooms. The second floor contains a terrace, a kitchen, and restrooms. The SHRDA benefited the community greatly through the years. The new library was an especially fitting, final gift from this agency.[18]

VIII

Reclaiming the Vision

*"Accommodate the needs of all income groups for quality housing
and facilitate the construction of the maximum number of
housing units for all income levels"*
—*from Goals, 2013–2021 Housing Element of the General Plan*

Signal Hill was planned as a residential community at the beginning
of the 1900s. The discovery of oil intruded on that vision and forever
changed the community. After achieving the dream of turning oil-
field land into thriving commercial property with the Auto Center
and Town Center plans, community leaders turned to the equally
daunting challenge of creating housing from scratch. By the 1970s,
the Hilltop had the appearance of a layer cake, having been graded
to suit oil production. In order to tame the Hilltop, the City would
need a plan for residential development in the oil field, and it would
need to be a plan that remained economically viable. Issues were
many: City officials would need to deal with the legacy environmental issues of the oil field, from the well abandonments to soil remediation to planning around active oil wells. The City would also have
to consolidate the dozens of communications antenna arrays that
dotted the Hilltop. Just as important, the City would need to construct the backbone utilities and amenities necessary to support residential development.

To begin, the City declared a moratorium on development in the
Hilltop district, to prevent willy-nilly development and allow time for

preparation of a comprehensive plan. Twenty-one years of collecting data, considering alternatives, and waiting for the right moment culminated in the adoption of the Hilltop Specific Plan. The result of the plan would be high-quality market-rate residential development, which in many cases took advantage of the spectacular views. The City would also embark on an ambitious park development plan to add active and passive recreational opportunities for all residents. In addition to the Hilltop Specific Plan, the Signal Hill Redevelopment Agency (SHRDA) was hard at work providing affordable housing, and the

The Signal Hill Redevelopment Agency was formed in 1974 as the City began to consider revitalization plans. Council member Gertrude Beebe is pictured next to one of the City's entry signs in the early 1970s. (Courtesy of City of Signal Hill.)

City was approving a wide variety of housing throughout the community. Along the way, the oil field became one of the most desirable places to live in Southern California, providing a range of housing opportunities to families of all income levels. This is quite the success story for a community of 2.2 square miles.

Antenna Consolidation: Cutting Down One Forest and Moving Another

By 1921, Signal Hill was known as "Porcupine Hill" based on the view of hundreds of silhouetted oil derricks sticking up on the Hilltop. And print publications of the time referred to the Hill as a "forest of derricks." The original wooden derricks were needed to drill for oil and were left in place to provide periodic servicing to the wells. During well servicing, long strings of oil pipe were removed from the well bore and the well pump serviced; some of the strings reached thousands of feet below the surface. The derricks facilitated this labor-intensive process. Wooden derricks turned into fire hazards, as attested by dozens of derrick fires, so steel derricks began to replace wooden derricks in the late 1920s. Then metal derricks were phased out in the 1960s and 1970s when mobile oil-well servicing trucks began to be more widely used.

As the derricks were removed, another collection of towers was revealed on the Hilltop—communication towers or antennas, which took advantage of the Hill's superior elevation. Over the many

This view of Signal Hill was taken from a helicopter looking to the north, c. 1960s. The civic center is in the lower middle of the photo. By that time, many of the wooden and steel derricks had been removed. By the 1960s, there were over nineteen radio and communication antenna arrays on the Hilltop, which in time interfered with development of residences. The City undertook a comprehensive plan to consolidate all of the antenna arrays into two main antennas, one operated by the City of Long Beach and the other by the Spanish Broadcasting Corporation. (Courtesy of City of Signal Hill.)

decades, the City had allowed the construction of individual towers and multiple towers, in what were termed "antenna farms." One of the original towers, at 2411 Skyline Drive, was owned and operated by the federal government as a communications antenna during World War II. The antenna was eventually sold in 1956, and housed KNOB—97.9 FM—the first all-jazz radio station in the nation. The tower was later purchased by the Spanish Broadcasting System (SBS). Cal State Long Beach continued the jazz tradition by operating a regionally known jazz station from this antenna under the call letters KKJZ.

The Hilltop housed a virtual smorgasbord of communications firms, including General Telephone, Mobilcom, and Advanced Communications. Eventually, the Hill was dotted with at least nineteen antenna arrays. Public entities relied on the antennas, including the

The Signal Hill water tank was a regional landmark for decades on the Hilltop. The tank was located on leased land and was demolished in the early 2000s as part of the construction of new water reservoirs on the Hilltop. The tower was festooned with communication antennas and microwave dishes, serving various government entities, like the Long Beach Unified School District, c. 1990. (Courtesy of City of Signal Hill.)

Long Beach Unified School District and the City of Signal Hill, who attached antennas to the City's water tank. The City of Long Beach operated a small radio tower in the 1930s at 2321 Stanley Avenue. Long Beach then constructed a 130-foot-tall tower in 1954 located on the same property. At that time, the use was listed "as permitted," and only a building permit was required. The tower was replaced by a 153-foot-tall tower in 1997. The new Long Beach tower had been constructed without zoning approvals or a building permit from the City of Signal Hill, with Long Beach claiming that as a government, they were exempt from permits.

The City noted, in the Hilltop Area Specific Plan, that the large number and locations of the antennas complicated future Hilltop development plans. The City identified the need to consolidate the antennas in a cluster around the City of Long Beach and Spanish Broadcasting System properties. The plan called for the public communication uses to be consolidated into the City of Long Beach antenna, and the private communications companies to be consolidated into the SBS antenna. The future Hilltop would have only two large towers, with space for multiple antennas, as opposed to over nineteen towers. Yet the consolidation was controversial. The City of Long Beach opposed the consolidation of the private companies into the adjacent SBS tower, arguing that these users would interfere with public safety transmissions. However, studies were completed, and the permits were eventually issued by the City.

The relocation began in two phases. In 1999, several private entities consolidated into the SBS antenna, along with KKJZ. By 2000, the City's water tower (which contained Long Beach Unified School District and the City of Signal Hill antennas) was demolished and the communication uses were relocated to the Long Beach antenna, and two additional antenna farms relocated to the SBS tower. These consolidations were spurred by the development of the Hilltop Village Residential Development (currently known as The Promontory). It is difficult to visualize the Hilltop today if all of the earlier towers had remained in place. A new tradition was started in 2002 when the City of Long Beach approached the City of Signal Hill with the idea of decorating the Long Beach tower for the Christmas holidays. Now, community members anticipate the lighting of the tower to welcome the season.[1]

Taming the Residential Development Plan

In 1986, the City initiated what would turn out to be the first of several attempts to reduce the Hilltop residential density, which had taken off with its approved high-density development of the 1974 General Plan. From 1974 to 1984, over 1,000 units of townhomes and condominiums were constructed in the SHRDA project area, many in the Hilltop oil-field area, which had been zoned for high density development. The rapid development of the Hilltop created controversies. Besides the overall density of the zoning, the residents expressed concern over the lack of on-site parking and the blocking of views from the new development. By the time of the 1986

Signal Hill aerial views, c. 1970s. In the 1980s and early 1990s, large residential condominium and townhome projects were starting to flank the Hilltop and a few larger residential developments had been constructed on the Hilltop itself. A wholesale rethinking of the Hilltop would trigger a development moratorium and several iterations of the Hilltop Specific Plan. (Courtesy of City of Signal Hill.)

Active oil wells and homes are neighbors, 2015.

General Plan, public concerns over high density resulted in reductions of Hilltop densities to thirty units per acre. The 1989 Land Use Element recognized that even this reduction was insufficient, and densities were lowered again to twenty-one units per acre over a 108-acre area. The contentiousness came to a head when Irvine-based Southwest Diversified announced its plans to construct 1,279 units on the Hilltop in spring 1990.

The City quickly adopted a development moratorium, effective May 1990. Then, by August, Southwest Diversified filed a lawsuit against the City. Fallout from the development moratorium, litigation, infighting between developers, and negotiations with the oil companies took the rest of the year to resolve. The City negotiated with the developer, and by that December, a settlement agreement allowed the developer to explore three alternative options—500, 700, or 900 units—with a backup plan should the City not approve any of the options. After consideration of the alternative plans, the City adopted the backup plan in August 1992. It consisted of 525 units, with 100 units on land not owned by the developer.

In March 1994, Southwest Diversified left the City, and Coscan-Davidson Homes stepped in as master developer. The operation of the oil field and the surface rights continued to be an issue with Signal Hill Petroleum. Litigation was filed in June 1994 between Coscan and Signal Hill Petroleum over which company would be the "managing partner" of the development. This litigation was not resolved until 1999, after which Hilltop construction began in earnest.[2]

During the 1990 Hilltop moratorium, ninety new homes were constructed, as part of the California Crown neighborhood, south of the Hilltop area. This subdivision demonstrated that high-quality, lower-density residential homes were very marketable. This subdivision is remarkable for another reason; it was the first residential

The City quickly adopted a development moratorium in August of 1990, which was followed by litigation and the development of alternative plans. This exhibit illustrates a 500-unit plan option. (Courtesy of City of Signal Hill.)

development to be designed around functioning oil wells. At present, the neighborhood preserves five operating wells, located on future residential lots and immediately adjacent to homes. Special care was taken to design the oil lots to minimize impacts. Gone are the overhead pumping units; rather, special subterranean pumps were installed.[3]

However, the lack of infrastructure dating back to the oil-field boom years continued to hamper the redevelopment of the Hilltop. Three small water tanks, dating from the 1920s and 1930s, served the neighborhood. Engineers determined that the water system was inadequate to service the area, and in 1999 the City embarked on a $10 million upgrade. The bond-funded improvements included constructing a new reservoir, with the 1.2-million-gallon tank located under Hilltop Park, as well as constructing the 1.3-million-gallon Temple Avenue Reservoir. The City also installed over 150,000 feet of new water pipelines and three pump stations.[4]

During a four-year period beginning in 2001, 246 homes were constructed in the Hilltop area, and 68 "infill" units were constructed on the East side of the Hill on lots that existed from the Denni 1904 subdivision. These lots had been used for oil production since the 1920s. The Bixby Ridge subdivision of 189 homes, adjacent to but not part of the Hilltop Plan, began construction in 2001. This large property was one of the remaining land holdings owned by the Bixby family. As a tribute to the family, the streets in the subdivision are named after historical Bixby family members. Several oil wells are also integrated into the neighborhood, and there was major relocation of oil utilities.

The Hilltop Area Specific Plan of 1993 was amended numerous times. In 2005, geotechnical studies revealed that active earthquake faults traversed the development site, and the plan was further amended. The planning area was constructed in phases and eventually resulted in construction of 262 homes. The Hilltop subdivisions learned the lessons from the California Crown neighborhood and incorporated active oil wells in open-space areas, including Hilltop Park and Discovery Well Park. The north slope of the Hill remains undeveloped, with 120 units anticipated for this area. The 1962 General Plan had forecast that the City would grow to 23,728 in population; however, the State listed Signal Hill's population in 2014 at only 11,411.

Although approved in 1994, it was not until 1999 that construction would begin on the Hilltop. The Comstock-Crosser development began in 2000. The Newport–Inglewood Fault played a role in further reducing the density to 441 residences, due primarily to the State requirements to set structures back from the fault line. (Courtesy of City of Signal Hill.)

Reclaiming a Historic Neighborhood: The Crescent Heights Story

Fortunately, City leaders were starting to realize the community's historical significance and were beginning to consider preservation possibilities. It was not until the 1960s that urban planners began to embrace historic preservation and to understand that conserving older buildings and historic places was important to a community's culture and population. Early American preservation efforts focused on saving buildings of consequence, such as George Washington's Mount Vernon, where preservation started in the 1850s. The effort to preserve colonial Williamsburg began in 1927 with a single donation from the Rockefeller Foundation to preserve just one building. This initial investment was just the beginning: over 301 acres of the town were preserved and restored over time, as a powerful demonstration of sound historic preservation. In 1949, the National Trust for Historic

In 2006, Ken Davis and the Signal Hill Historical Society collaborated on the book Images of America: Signal Hill. *The publication is an invaluable source of historic photographs of the community. This picture from the book shows the Crescent Heights neighborhood prior to the discovery of oil. Most of the homes pictured here were destroyed with the onslaught of oil production; however, the dark house in the center exists to this day. It, along with a handful of original surviving homes, would become the seeds for the City's historic district. (Courtesy of Signal Hill Historical Society.)*

Oil Wells, Signal Hill District, Long Beach, Cal.

Crescent Heights neighborhood. Western Publishing Company in Los Angeles produced dozens of Signal Hill postcards in the 1920s and 1930s. The postcards were popular with tourists who visited the oil field and were often labeled the "The Famous Signal Hill, Long Beach, California."

Preservation adopted a specific set of goals for historic preservation, and in the 1960s, urban planning programs began teaching a future generation of planners about the value of historic preservation to communities. Currently, over thirty major universities offer degrees in historic preservation. In addition, many local communities now have historic preservation departments and staff, as well as active historical societies and conservancies.

Historic preservation at the neighborhood level requires motivated property owners who see the value in preserving their properties. In the early 2000s, the Crescent Heights neighborhood offered an opportunity for Signal Hill to collaborate with its residents to preserve a historic neighborhood. The Crescent Heights neighborhood consists of several blocks, bounded by Cherry Avenue on the east and Walnut Street on the west, and generally located between Burnett Street and Willow Street. The area had originally been subdivided for the construction of individual homes, but like much of Signal Hill, the neighborhood was overrun with oil production in the 1920s. Even though oil production took over the neighborhood, some homes were of high enough caliber that they were not demolished.

As the oil production declined and oil facilities were dismantled, it became clear to the City and the property owners that the original historic fabric of the neighborhood was worth preserving and enhancing.

By 2002, the City adopted the Crescent Heights Historic District Specific Plan to protect the existing historic buildings in the new historic district and to provide an architectural theme for historic buildings relocated into the area. The plan was also designed to guide new construction to be consistent with the architectural character of Southern California from the 1890s through the 1930s. Similar to how Signal Hill needed to reconstruct its Town Center, the community needed to reconstruct this historic neighborhood. In Ken Davis's book *Images of America: Signal Hill*, readers can find vintage Crescent Heights photographs of original homes and of the damage caused by the oil industry as well as pictures of the efforts to

Signal Hill has worked to reclaim its residential neighborhoods from oil production, and interest in historic preservation has grown over the years. This historic home was saved from the wrecking ball and relocated from Long Beach. Originally adjacent to the ocean front in Long Beach, it was threatened with demolition for a new condominium development. It became the first historic home relocated into the Crescent Heights Historic District. (Courtesy of Signal Hill Historical Society.)

reclaim the neighborhood. There are also photographs of a historic home being relocated from Long Beach to Crescent Heights in the mid-2000s. The Crescent Heights plan would also be used to guide the architecture and planning of Town Center West shopping center, the Crescent Square project, and the Heritage Square Mixed-Use Project.[5]

The Unplanned Development Moratorium: State Changes Well Abandonment Standards

Soon after the 1908 invention of the Model T sent the nation into a petroleum frenzy, it became apparent to the State of California that potential dangers needed to be addressed. Early legislative action in the area of minerals—from the appointment of an Honorary State Geologist in 1851 to the creation of a State Mining Bureau in 1880—had focused almost exclusively on gold, and on surveying and collecting data. With the petroleum boom, compiling information was not enough. In 1915, the legislature created a State Oil and Gas Supervisor position and a Division of Oil and Gas within the Mining Bureau (with an expanded mission, it would later become the Division of Oil, Gas and Geothermal Resources, DOGGR, within the Department of Conservation). They were formed to track hundreds of oil fields, issue drilling permits, and inspect wells for cement plugs and water shut-off valves. These plugs and shut-off valves were necessary to protect the groundwater aquifer.

The need to protect the aquifer was urgent. The southeastern area of Los Angeles—where Signal Hill and Long Beach were located—had depended on groundwater wells for drinking water, agriculture, and industry up until 1939 when the Colorado River Aqueduct opened. Meanwhile, deeper wells and a receding water table created a vicious cycle, and residents became uneasy about their future access to water, especially with the population growing so rapidly. The entangled relationship of water and petroleum was demonstrated in 1918, when farmers in nearby Santa Fe Springs deepened their water wells and struck oil instead.

Deep drilling always creates the possibility of polluting groundwater, by creating avenues for contaminants such as oil to reach previously sealed aquifers. A particular danger came from wells that had been abandoned, because they either came up dry or became played out. Before the 1920s, there were no formal standards for the abandonment of oil wells. Sometimes, telephone poles and soil were packed into abandoned wells as rough plugs; this, however, created the potential of leaking methane and crude oil. Beginning in the 1920s, the State adopted various well-abandonment standards as technology advanced, the understanding of geology moved forward, and practices were improved to control leaking methane and oil. By 1989, the State had adopted a comprehensive site-plan review process to permit well abandonments. The standards required plugs at various depths in the wells to prohibit methane and oil from reaching the surface or contaminating groundwater aquifers. And, although the standards encouraged setting structures back from closed wells, it also allowed structures, including homes, to be constructed atop a properly abandoned oil well.

At its peak, over 1,719 wells existed in the 2.2-square-mile city, but only 421 were actively pumping in 2010. The concentration of oil wells and the prior small-lot land subdivisions made it virtually impossible to develop portions of the oil field without abandoning wells. Financial institutions were reluctant to finance developments in the oil field without a government-approved well-abandonment permit. The State's well-abandonment permit process had worked for the last sixty years: there were no reports of either leaking methane or oil from previously abandoned wells.

Despite this track record, the State halted their abandonment permits abruptly in 2010, when the well-abandonment process was discontinued by DOGGR. This sudden change affected every oil field in the state where redevelopment was taking place. The "de facto development moratorium" imposed by the State would last over four years and impact all development in and adjacent to the oil field. Prior to 2010, Signal Hill's oil code relied upon the State's well-abandonment permits to allow development in the oil field, and no alternative process was in place when DOGGR halted its permits. Signal Hill development came to a grinding halt. One developer, EDCO, was already constructing its new refuse transfer station on California Avenue over seven abandoned oil wells. In order to keep the project moving, creative engineering was employed when EDCO agreed to redesign the transfer station with a removable roof, so that in the event an abandoned well leaked, they could remove a portion of the roof and bring in a service truck to re-abandon the well. However, not all developers had the land area or a large enough building footprint to accommodate well abandonment and continue development.

The late 1980s State abandonment standards were developed in part to protect groundwater from being contaminated by oil field drilling. When abandoning an oil well, the driller needed to place plugs at the base of fresh water, so that oil would not travel up from the hydrocarbon producing zones to mix with groundwater. Oil fields are typically divided into producing zones or strata. DOGGR required plugs at these zones and at the bottom of the well. In theory, this was the preferred plan of action; however, in practice, some oil wells were so damaged that the driller could not reach the bottom of the well or place plugs at the various hydrocarbon zones due to obstructions, broken pipes, or earth movement that crushed the pipes. One residential development along Pacific Coast Highway was required to re-abandon an oil well. After investing over one million dollars in the effort, they gave up and redesigned the project, losing residential units in the process.

The City struggled to adopt various interim measures in 2011, 2012, and 2013, while comprehensive studies were completed to assess the environmental issues and to propose solutions. The City retained a series of oil-field experts to confirm that the City's interim oil code was more protective of the environment than the State's codes. In February 2014, under the direction of Susan Paulsen, PhD, the firm of Flow Sciences completed one of the first comprehensive reviews of water contamination in oil fields, and determined that oil drilling had little impact on the water quality within the drinking-water aquifers in the Signal Hill Field. Then, in December 2014, Susan Mearns, PhD, of Mearns Consulting, found that the methane protection systems that the City required to be installed in structures

protected public health and safety. New well-abandonment standards were developed by Evans & Walker, experts in oil field controls
and development. These studies led to the City adopting the 2015 oil
code and well-abandonment standards. Four long years of development uncertainty and chaos had finally come to an end.[6]

Parks for the Community and the Region

Creating parks and recreational opportunities were a high prior-
ity for the many city councils over the decades. Only six years after
incorporation, the City completed the purchase of the estate of Jessie
Nelson, where the new city hall would be constructed in 1934. The
City constructed Hinshaw Park on the ten acres of the Nelson Estate
that were not used for the city hall and the police and fire station.
Eventually, the name of the park was changed to Signal Hill Park, and
it remains the City's largest.

Hinshaw Park served the community located south of the oil
field; however, a park was needed to serve residents north of the oil
field, south of Wardlow Road. The 2.78-acre Reservoir Park was the
next park constructed for this area, which was called the "silk stock-
ing" neighborhood since it had concrete sidewalks. These two parks
served the community into the 1970s, when new residential development started on the Hilltop. The mini-park, .54-acre Hillbrook Park,
was constructed by the SHRDA in 1986 to serve the southeastern
area of the community.

The City went on a park-building spree in the late 1990s through
the 2010s. The crown jewel of the City's park system in this period
was Hilltop Park, constructed in 1999. *See California*, a travel guide,
described it as one of the "most interesting parks in California."
The 3.2-acre park sits atop a buried 1.2 million-gallon reservoir that
services a major part of the City with water. The park also includes
active oil wells, and artwork by Jon Cicchetti, Tom Weir, and Craig
Cree Stone. It is left up to interpretation, but there is a mist tower
in the center of the park, said to be evocative of either the smoke
signals from the Native Americans using the Hilltop or an oil gusher
from bygone days. There are also the "shadow art frames," which tell
the story of the history of Signal Hill, and the Friends of the Signal

Hilltop Park, which opened in 1999 and was constructed atop a 1.2-million-gallon water reservoir. This photo shows the Hilltop prior to the development of the Promontory and other Hilltop subdivisions. (Courtesy of City of Signal Hill.)

Hill Library installed the Millennial Brick Project around the mist tower area. Building Hilltop Park was a major decision by the city council, since the City bears the expense of maintaining what is in reality a high-use regional park.

The next park established was the 4.9-acre Discovery Well Park, built in the area adjacent to the Discovery Well, Alamitos No. 1, which contains the California State historic marker and the still-pumping Discovery Well. The park was constructed by the Alamitos Land Company and then dedicated to the City as part of the Bixby Ridge development project. Rubble, from the Long Beach earthquake and from years of oil company use, was encountered during construction and needed to be removed and remediated. The park also contains active oil wells, alongside basketball courts, picnic areas, a small field, and a community center.

As part of the general plan in the 1990s, the City also envisioned a series of trails linking the various parks with parts of the entire community. However, the vision would need several years to come to fruition. The Los Angeles County Board of Supervisors placed a park funding measure, Proposition A, on the 1996 ballot. It passed and resulted in the Safe Neighborhood Parks Act of 1996. This act

Sweeping panoramic views from Hilltop Park.

Once an oil field, Discovery Well Park now welcomes residents with recreational and open green spaces.

Panorama Promenade

Calbrisas Park

Raymond Arbor Park

Sunset View Park

Tribute to the Roughnecks *depicts Signal Hill Petroleum Chairman Jerry Barto and Shell Oil employee Bruce Kerr installing pipe, as a commemoration of those who worked the rigs in Signal Hill's earlier years. The statue, by sculptor Cindy Jackson, was donated by Signal Hill Petroleum and is located on Skyline Drive.*

provided funding to each community for park development and established a grant program for large regional projects.

Signal Hill applied for a competitive grant at the urging of then–Community Development Director Gary Jones to construct a series of walking trails throughout the Hilltop. It took over a decade of working on the system, with the Panorama Promenade becoming the first of several trails on the Hilltop. The Panorama Promenade is a linear park that follows the former oil field road—Panorama Avenue—which was closed to vehicular traffic in the 1990s. The former road was converted into a walking trail with six view points of the region—looking west, north, and east. The promenade has exercise stations as well as seating areas that have historic photos and narratives of the community.

Due to the expense of purchasing land and demolishing homes, the City concentrated on adding mini-parks to various neighborhoods from around 2000 to 2010. The SHRDA participated in the construction of the .5-acre Calbrisas Park, which has an open field, half-court basketball court, and fence artwork by Jon Cicchetti called *California Breezes*. This park was opened along with the Calbrisas housing development. Another mini-park constructed with the assistance of the SHRDA was Raymond Arbor Park. This .33-acre park features a playground for young children, and a fountain and seating area celebrating a former resident who kept dozens of colorful birds.

The area has a memorial, decorative entry in her honor. Sunset View Park is located on Skyline Drive adjacent to Hilltop Park; it features artwork and a solar calendar. The most recent park constructed was the City's first dog park. The .46-acre park includes separate areas for large and small dogs. The dog park was the culmination of several years of planners and community service staff working to find an appropriate location. Located on land purchased by the SHRDA at 3100 California Avenue, it opened in March 2018.[7]

The Search for Affordable Housing: It Can and Must Be Done

California has long faced the question of how best to construct affordable housing, as rents soar and many of the state's residents cannot afford to purchase a home. Signal Hill is a case example of how affordable housing can be done. Housing production and affordability has ebbed and flowed in California over the decades, impacted by natural disasters like earthquakes and fires, the Great Depression and the Great Recession, and the economic booms of World War II, as well as more recent examples of the rise of the technology economy in San Francisco, and in Los Angeles's Silicon Beach. Government-provided affordable housing programs grew out of the Great Depression and have changed through the years to meet needs, budgets, and perspectives.

Providing affordable housing in Los Angeles County has been a historic problem, with each wave of migrants and immigrants overwhelming the available housing stock. Los Angeles County was home to 170,298 residents in 1900. Ten years later the County had grown to 504,131 residents. By 1930, there were 2,208,492 residents. Growth slowed somewhat during the Great Depression; however, at the beginning of the 1940s, the County registered 2,785,643 residents. Labor was needed to service the defense industries during World War II, and by 1950 the County was inhabited by 4,151,687 residents. The County's population was 7,032,075 by the time Signal Hill decision makers were considering forming the redevelopment agency in the early 1970s.

The City of Long Beach's growth followed a similar trajectory. Growth took off in the 1920s, with the discovery of oil. Throughout the region, roughnecks migrated to oil fields like Signal Hill's. Tent cities arose instantly. State Historian Kevin Starr wrote that, overnight in Signal Hill, "Thousands of men poured in, looking for jobs; and in their wake arrived the prostitutes competing for scarce bungalows, together with speakeasy operators and their bootleg suppliers."[8] The discovery of oil resulted in a building boom in Long Beach, with the City reporting $1 million per month in building activity in 1922. In 1930, Long Beach had 142,032 residents and grew to 250,767 by 1950. Long Beach was given the nickname "Iowa by the Sea" due to the influx of Midwesterners from early- to mid-century. At its first official census after cityhood in 1930, Signal Hill had a population of 2,932 residents. It grew to 4,040 residents by 1950.

Housing availability became an acute problem in the aftermath of the 1933 Long Beach earthquake. The magnitude 6.3 quake was reported to have killed 115 people and injured over 2,000, as buildings crumbled. Reports published by the National Board of Fire Underwriters revealed that over 20,000 homes were damaged in the region, damage ranging from cracked plaster to complete destruction.[9] Dorothy Wise recalled that she drove around Long Beach with her mother after the quake to survey the damage. "The part that fascinated me was the apartments. The front was just sheared off, and you could see the bathtubs and toilets, and to me that was just shocking."[10]

The Long Beach earthquake came at the depths of the Great Depression. The economic upheaval exposed the disparities between the wealthy and the poor, with the disinvestment in housing creating slums in Los Angeles and other communities. It was estimated that in 1930, 20% of the housing in Los Angeles County was unfit for human habitation; 30% had no indoor toilets, and 20% had no bathtubs. National housing issues of the time resulted in Congress passing the United States Housing Act of 1937 (Wagner–Steagall Act). The Act created a US Housing Authority, which could make loans to local housing agencies. The City of Los Angeles and Los Angeles County collaborated in the creation of a joint housing authority in 1938. Its Carmelitos Housing Project was Southern California's first affordable housing complex, and was located in north

172 | *Black Gold in Paradise*

Long Beach at 5150 Atlantic Boulevard. The project began construction in 1939 and was a massive project of 607 affordable units in 67 buildings spread over 50 acres of land, at a cost of $2.6 million in 1940. Soon, other projects were under construction in the county, including Ramona Gardens, which replaced what was known as the Beaudry Street slum.

With the nation's entry into World War II, the housing shortage was again exacerbated. By 1943, over 200,000 Los Angeles County residents were employed in the defense industry. State assembly member Ernest Debs commented that Long Beach "was wholly unprepared" for the influx of workers. The lack of housing impacted the war effort, with service members having to live far from the naval and army bases in the region. Housing was so scarce that families resorted to sharing homes. By the early 1950s, affordable housing was in such short supply that one Long Beach affordable housing project had a waiting list of eight hundred families.

Finally, in 1988, the state legislature acknowledged the problem and took action. Until that time, redevelopment agencies (RDAs) were not required to provide affordable housing. This changed with the adoption of AB 4566, known as the Polonco Act. The act mandated that RDAs set aside 20% of their annual revenues into a Low–Moderate Income Housing Fund (LMIHF) and use these funds to promote affordable housing. A further reform in 1993 provided for the termination of RDAs should they not use their LMIHF funds. From 2001 to 2008, RDAs statewide created 63,600 new affordable units. But the State dissolved the RDAs in 2011, bringing an untimely halt to what had grown to be a massive program. According to the state controller, at the time there was a total of $1.02 billion remaining in the program, from annual set-asides intended for affordable housing in 595 project areas. Just in the next two years, from January 2012 to December 2013, RDAs were planning to construct 12,050 units. At one time, California had the most robust affordable housing construction program in the nation as a result of community redevelopment agency activities. Needless to say, there were dire consequences to the production of affordable housing when the State dissolved the redevelopment agencies.[11]

The Sad Legacy of Racial and Housing Discrimination

Housing discrimination went hand in hand with the housing shortage. Whole neighborhoods were "redlined," and deed restrictions prevented non-whites from purchasing property. Entire books have been written on the historic problems of housing discrimination throughout the Los Angeles Region. At one time, Chinese and Japanese citizens could not purchase property in California. The federal 1933 Home Owners' Loan Corporation, part of the New Deal initiative in response to the Great Depression, specified where black Americans and other minorities could or could not buy property with government assistance. The HOLC's 1939 "redlining" map of central Los Angeles County shows the entire boundaries of Signal Hill as reserved for white Americans, including the oil fields and industrial areas as well as residential sections.

California's Unruh Civil Rights Act, enacted in 1959, attempted to deal with housing discrimination by stating that "all persons within the jurisdiction of the state are free and equal, and entitled to the full and equal accommodation, advantages, facilities and privileges or services in all business establishments of any kind whatsoever." Discrimination problems continued, resulting in Governor Pat Brown declaring that the State must formulate solutions to create more low-income housing. The legislature passed the Fair Housing Act of 1963, prohibiting property owners from discriminating based on "ethnicity, religion, sex, marital status, physical handicap, or familial status."

The California Real Estate Association was incensed by the Fair Housing Act and sponsored Proposition 14 on the statewide ballot in 1964. The measure read in part that "Neither the State nor any subdivision or agency thereof shall deny, limit or abridge, directly or indirectly, the right of any person, who is willing or desires to sell, lease or rent any portion or all of his real property, to decline to sell, lease or rent such property to such person or persons as he, in his absolute discretion chooses." The initiative passed with a two-to-one vote, but it was dismissed as unconstitutional by the US Supreme Court in 1966. A new form of discrimination surfaced, called "block busting." Real estate agents would go into predominantly white areas and convince residents that minorities were moving in following the Supreme Court's dismissal of Proposition 14. White families would sell their properties at significantly lower prices, and the agents turned around and sold the properties to black families at substantially higher prices.

The sad legacy of racial segregation and discrimination was of course not confined to Signal Hill. The surrounding city of Long Beach began to address the issues in 1964, with formation of the Fair Housing Corporation, devoted to "fair and open housing practices" in the community. The FHC started a series of anti-discrimination lawsuits as soon as the Supreme Court overturned Proposition 14. The FHC investigated over 200 apartment complexes in Long Beach and found that 114 buildings, representing 1,450 units, practiced racially discriminatory practices. The investigative reports were sent to the US Department of Justice, Housing Section, Civil Rights Division. The DOJ eventually decided, in 1972, to send officers to issue warnings to the property owners instead of filing lawsuits. The FHC continued to pursue landlords who discriminated, with their own litigation based on State laws, and won landmark cases. Housing barriers eventually began to fall in Signal Hill as well, and the City's housing accomplishments are now a source of pride and inclusion.[12]

The Vision: Bringing Dignity to Residents

During the State's commitment to affordable and special-needs housing through RDAs, the Signal Hill Redevelopment Agency (SHRDA) ambitiously pursued the program's goals. The first project carried out was Eucalyptus Gardens—a twenty-four-unit development designed for disabled persons and constructed in 1994. The SHRDA provided financial assistance of $1 million in the form of a land contribution. Also in the mid-nineties, Deputy City Manager Debbie Rich convinced Mayor Tina Hansen and the city council to use redevelopment funds to purchase some property that was for sale on the open real estate market to construct an affordable housing development. It was an area with market-rate housing, but housing that was poorly designed and in a state of deterioration and

A Las Brisas housing unit.

disrepair. The resulting development, Las Brisas, was ultimately constructed in two phases, and was located on both sides of California Avenue, north of 24th Street. It was built with the help of the 20% set-aside in the Low–Moderate Income Housing Fund. The project also relied on federal assistance in the form of a capital grant for supportive housing for people with disabilities.

Hansen and the council insisted that they did not want to just build an affordable housing development for low-income families and seniors, but they wanted to build a community. The City envisioned a park, a community center, and a police substation within the project, along with a child-care center and a senior center constructed with foundation grants. Las Brisas Community Housing Phase I was the City's second SHRDA project (after Eucalyptus Gardens) and in the end, its largest—a ninety-two-unit acquisition and rehabilitation project consisting of sixty-two two-bedroom and twenty-eight three-bedroom units. The project took several years to plan and complete, especially since it required land assembly over a three-block area and the use of eminent domain on several of the properties.

The total cost for Las Brisas Phase I was $18 million, and other funding sources were required beyond SHRDA, including $2 million from the Los Angeles County Community Development Commission; a $2 million HELP loan, which was repaid by the RDA; $8 million in State tax credits; and $500,000 from the State's Affordable Housing Program fund. The $1.7 million community center was funded by private foundations, including the Mark S. Taper Foundation, the Ralph M. Parsons Foundation, the Weingart Foundation, and the Ahmanson Foundation. The $522,000 Calbrisas Park was funded by a State grant and the City of Signal Hill. The SHRDA invested a total of $6 million in the project. The SHRDA's contribution included $5 million for site assembly and relocation costs, and a loan of $150,000 to the developer. Las Brisas Phase I was completed in 2004 and consisted of twenty-three renovated fourplex units.

Encouraged by the success of Las Brisas Phase I, the RDA moved on to Phase II, which consisted of a four-story, sixty-unit family project. The project was constructed on the former right of way for the San Pedro, Los Angeles & Salt Lake Railroad, on the east side of California Avenue. After many years of groundwork and building, completion of the Las Brisas Community Housing Development Phase II was celebrated in September 2007. Approximately seventy people attended the official grand opening, where Mayor Hansen noted that when Signal Hill embarked on the project in 2002, several community leaders spoke out against it, saying it could not be done by a small city. "We have proven that not only can it be done, but it must be done," stated Hansen. State Senator Alan Lowenthal went a step further, observing "This is a model for community revitalization . . .. Everybody in the State government should take a trip through here to see what can be done to develop affordable housing."

The once-blighted neighborhood had been completely transformed. Original units constructed in the 1950s were demolished to make way for the new housing development. The earlier complex was constructed with limited parking, and the five-block area was well maintained while it was used by naval personnel. Then the Long Beach Naval Base was closed, and the neighborhood went rapidly downhill, with dozens of the buildings owned by absentee landlords. Mayor Hansen described the neighborhood in 1994 as rundown residences with garbage and other refuse strewn through the grounds

The Zinnia community.

Left to right: Council Member Tina Hansen, Los Angeles County Supervisor Janice Hahn, Mayor Edward Wilson, Vice Mayor Lori Woods and Council Member Larry Forester at the Zinnia opening.

and streets, broken-down and seemingly abandoned vehicles, and the overshadowing presence of criminal elements. "It was a very frightening place back then," Hansen recalled.

The SHRDA's final affordable housing project under the RDA program was the Zinnia Affordable Housing Community. This seventy-two-unit low-income housing development also took several years to plan and construct. The four-story project carried out the community design principles pioneered at Las Brisas, including open space and a playground, community center, computer lab, community garden, and fenced area for dogs. The project was funded through the State's tax credit program.

Asked for a comment on the project, Council Member Tina Hansen stated that the quality of the Zinnia Affordable Housing Community "brings dignity to residents that would make anyone

nt to live there." Based on these project successes, the city council believed that Governor Brown and the legislature were making
a shortsighted mistake by ending redevelopment in California to
help solve the State's budget crisis. The council expressed concern
that the unintended consequences would be to make housing less
affordable in California and to exacerbate the lack of new affordable
housing. Later, Senator Lowenthal commented that voting for the
act turned out to be his biggest mistake as a legislator.[13]

Money, Effort, Vision . . . and Success

Over the lifetime of California's local redevelopment agencies, some
of the various projects had earned the program a reputation for
manipulation and mismanagement. When the State shuttered the
initiative at the end of 2011, there were few mourners. For Signal Hill,
though, it is difficult to envision what the City would be without the
SHRDA's $102.2 million expenditure on behalf of the community.

Over $40.3 million went to assembling parcels for redevelop-
ment. The most ambitious of the programs included the acquisition
of hundreds of small-lot parcels in the former oil field, beginning
in 2007. This project eventually totaled $18 million and freed up
over twenty-five acres of land for future development, including
the entire Windemere Tract at the southeast corner of Atlantic Avenue and Spring Street, the former site of Julian Petroleum, and the
Richmond Field Absorption Plant fire property. At nearly every step,
developers encountered the legacy of town-lot drilling, from the
infamous days when residents literally drilled wells in their yards.

The "reabandonment" of ninety-six improperly closed wells—
beginning with the Auto Center project in 1989 and continuing
through 2011—called for sustained effort and expenditure of $7.7
million. The two shopping centers alone, Town Center East and
Town Center West, each required remediation of more than twenty-
five wells, along with careful planning to permit still-productive
wells to operate on the properties. Cleanup of contaminated soil
brought the cost to $15.1 million. Another $10.6 million was invested
in various infrastructure projects, including street widenings, intersection improvements, and sewer system upgrades. In the end, the

$100 million-plus from the SHRDA was supplemented by additional investment from other public and private sources.

Besides money, it required great patience, energy, and vision to accomplish every necessary task, and at the same time allow the oil field to continue producing profitably and responsibly. In the end, the Signal Hill Redevelopment Agency and the forward-thinking leaders who directed it had transformed some of the most damaged areas of the little city into affordable housing units, modern retail locations, playgrounds, a library, seven City parks, a police station, open spaces, a community garden, a dog park, a trail system . . . every necessity and amenity of a thriving, pleasant modern town—a paradise in the midst of the black gold.

Postscript

Jonathan Booth when he was interviewed by the City of Signal Hill in 1991. (Courtesy of City of Signal Hill.)

When Charles Booth told his young son, "That should change things up here, Jonny Boy," he was right to fear what the discovery of oil would mean for his peaceful little farming community. Oil ushered in a new era of prosperity for a few, heartbreak and financial ruin for some, relatively stable employment for others, and ecological devastation for the entire Hill. Despite his misgivings, Charles Booth went on to have his own wells by 1922. Like so many other families, the Booths suffered through the Great Depression, the Long Beach earthquake, and every trial to which their beloved community was subjected. Although Charles's paradise was lost for over sixty years, the community leaders rallied in what became a Herculean effort to rebuild the City from the ravages of oil.

Charles Booth died of a sudden heart attack in March 1941, leaving $50,000 in debt, which Jonathan worked to make good on.

Charles would not live to see Signal Hill's rebirth. Son Jonathan, too, was shaped by the history of Signal Hill. Like his father and so many others, he dabbled in oil speculation but found wealth elusive. During the war years, he worked as an engineer at the nearby Douglas Aircraft plant. He later worked for Hancock Oil, including in 1958 when its refinery burned to the ground. Between father and son, Charles and Jonathan Booth encapsulate more than a century of the often tumultuous history of Signal Hill.

Jonathan was thankful for being asked to participate in the City's oral history project. We today are lucky to have his recollections, and those of the eighteen others who participated in the project. Jonathan concluded his history by saying that the City was doing a "bang-up job" and that the City's future plans were "terrific." On June 23, 1921, Discovery Day, Charles Booth sensed that the coming transformation of Signal Hill might be for the worse. If he could come back for a visit, he might agree with his son—a bang-up job, and a terrific future.

Afterword

In my career as a city manager and city planner, I always felt it was important to bring a sense of history to the California communities I served. This has been easy in some communities, and harder in others.

As community development director for the City of La Verne, I found the citizens ready to preserve their historic downtown in 1982, with the adoption of the Old Town Specific Plan. A centerpiece of this effort was the preservation of Miller Hall, the historic former women's dormitory of the University of La Verne. The building was slated to be razed by the University, but as the city planning director, I denied the demolition permit, and in a controversial decision, the city council upheld the decision. When I moved on to the City of Downey, my good friend and mentor Steve Preston succeeded me, and continued to implement and improve the plan. Today Old Town La Verne, Miller Hall, and the University of La Verne campus are testaments to the importance of preserving our past.

Historic preservation was a harder sell in the City of Downey. As the assistant city manager, I worked on an inventory of the major historic homes, but historic preservation did not receive much attention from city council or the community at large. We did have one great success story—saving the oldest operating McDonald's, one of the original "Golden Arches." The Downey restaurant, opened in 1953 as a sit-outside hamburger stand, was the second restaurant owned by the original McDonald brothers, before Ray Kroc bought the fledgling chain. McDonald's corporation was ready to demolish the restaurant and replace it with a newer version, but the city council intervened. Eventually, the McDonald's corporation realized the importance of the historic store and the large "Speedee" pole sign, reconstructing the restaurant and even adding a museum alongside. This site is now one of Downey's major tourist attractions.

Then came a position as city manager of the City of South Pasadena, where I found a community eager to embrace their history. Working with a citizen's committee of architects, planners, and historic preservation experts, we completed a citywide historic inventory, and initiated the design of the Mission Street Specific Plan, with its centerpiece, the Mission Street Metro light rail station. Today the historic mixed-use Mission Street district is thriving, and is a tribute to my good friend Bill Campbell, who passed away a few years ago. As the community development director, Bill did more than anyone in the 1990s to promote this preservation initiative. I think of him often when I ride LA's Metro Gold Line train, or just enjoy the ambiance of the Mission Street neighborhood.

When I arrived in 1996 as Signal Hill's city manager, I was not sure about the interest in historic preservation. The history was very rich and interesting, but much of the historic fabric of the community had been ripped out by the rush to oil exploration and production. Fortunately, the city council recognized the importance of preservation. We were able to weave historic elements into a variety of projects. The Denni walls were incorporated into Hilltop Park and the surrounding residential neighborhoods. The Hilltop Park and Panorama Promenade paid homage to the varied history of the community. Discovery Well Park celebrated the success of oil in the community. The birds on the fence at Raymond Arbor Park celebrate one of the early residents of the neighborhood, and historic tiles adorn the walkways at Las Brisas Park. Crescent Heights and these other projects stand as a testament to the early vision of historically aware residential development.

"The most Beautiful Home Site in Southern California." That's the claim in a 1910 real estate brochure from the Signal Hill Improvement Company. That's advertising hyperbole, of course, and not something you're likely to hear any Signal Hill resident say without a wink. But in all earnestness, they can claim that Signal Hill is the place where, in a time of great need, the people came together and recovered their hometown from overwhelming challenges, earning its unofficial motto, "The little city that could and did."

Acknowledgments

A big thanks goes to former Deputy City Clerk Becky Burleson, who researched the life of Jessie Nelson as part of the City's initiative to name the new middle school after our first mayor. Becky also researched the actions by the board of trustees from 1924 through 1926. The 2013 paper "Three Views from the Hill: Signal Hill, California, 1910–2000" by Dr. Craig Hendricks of Long Beach Community College provided a wealth of historical research and source materials.

Information gathered as part of the City's 1991 oral history project also provided invaluable insights. Thanks to the Signal Hill Historical Society and the Signal Hill Library for their assistance in archival materials, and to the Huntington Library—an amazing resource with knowledgeable, helpful staff—as well as to the Historical Society of Long Beach and the Long Beach Library. A huge debt is due to Ken Davis, for his book *Images of America: Signal Hill*.

City staff members Anthony Caraveo and Chris St. Marie provided assistance in scanning archival materials and maps. Former City Manager Frank Baxter, had the foresight to collect five scrapbooks of materials on Signal Hill in the 1960s, with newspaper articles, photos, promotional brochures, and other materials that bring Signal Hill's history to life.

Special thanks to the Signal Hill City Council, City Manager Charlie Honeycutt, Community Development Director Scott Charney, Economic Development Manager Elise McCaleb, and Deputy City Clerk Kim Boles for their assistance with this book.

These acknowledgments would not be complete without thanking former City Attorney Dave Aleshire and Deputy City Attorney Sunny Soltani. Dave and Sunny worked tirelessly to help the City assemble the hundreds of parcels in the old oil field and to put them into productive uses. In writing this book, I have often consulted the extensive information they amassed from those efforts. I'm also grateful to Dave for sharing his unique perspective in the foreword to *Black Gold in Paradise*. In 2018 he celebrated forty years as Signal Hill's attorney—a remarkable run for a remarkable man.

A particular thanks to Populore Publishing Company, especially Rae Jean Sielen and Andrew Rorabaugh, for their invaluable editorial and production assistance.

Finally, I wish to thank the Historical Society of Southern California—together with underwriter Ahmanson Foundation—for providing funds to assist with publication of this book but also for extending grant recipient eligibility to independent and non-academic projects such as this one.

One of my aims in writing this book has been to assist Signal Hill—and other—city councils, managers, and planners in understanding the complex nature of land use reclamation and redevelopment. If I have succeeded to any degree, it is only through the help of these and so many other collaborators, colleagues, and supporters.

Photograph Credits

Unless noted otherwise, photographs are from author's personal collection.

p 13: Unknown photographer, public domain, University of Southern California Libraries, California Historical Society Collection, 1860–1960, https://commons. wikimedia.org/wiki/File:Close-up_of_a_specimen_of_lemons_and_blossoms_on_a_ branch_(CHS-1868).jpg.

p 17–19: Pacific Electric Railway Historical Society, www.peryhs.org.

p 36 (top): M. Kashower Co., Los Angeles, California. [No date or copyright info.]

p 44: View of oil fields around Los Angeles, Clarence and Edna Forncrook, 1922, retrieved from the Library of Congress, Maps, #2006627695.

p 45 (bottom): Western Publishing & Novelty Co., Los Angeles, California. [No date or copyright info.]

p 50 (bottom)–53: Courtesy of University of Southern California, on behalf of the USC Libraries Special Collections.

p 54–55: Ansel Adams, Ansel Adams Fortune Magazine Collection, Los Angeles Photographers Collection / Los Angeles Public Library.

p 56: Cemetery Statue and Oil Wells, Long Beach, California, 1939. Photograph by Ansel Adams. Collection Center for Creative Photography, University of Arizona. © The Ansel Adams Publishing Rights Trust.

p 64 (bottom): Unknown photographer, Security Pacific National Bank Photo Collection / Los Angeles Public Library.

p 81: Herman Schultheis, Herman J. Schultheis Collection, Los Angeles Photographers Collection / Los Angeles Public Library.

p 83: Herman Schultheis, Herman J. Schultheis Collection, Los Angeles Photographers Collection / Los Angeles Public Library.

p 95 (top): Doc Searls, Creative Commons Attribution—Share Alike 2.0 Generic. https://commons.wikimedia.org/wiki/File:Platform_A,_Dos_Cuadras_(1).jpg.

p 95 (bottom): Antandrus, Creative Commons Attribution—Share Alike 3.0 Unported. https://commons.wikimedia.org/wiki/File:Oil1969extent.jpg.

p 102: Los Angeles Daily News Negative Archive (Collection 1387). UCLA Library Special Collections, Charles E. Young Research Library, UCLA.

p 160: Western Publishing & Novelty Co., Los Angeles, California. [No date or copyright info.]

p 203–205: Views of oil fields around Los Angeles, *Clarence and Edna Forncrook, 1922, retrieved from the Library of Congress, Maps, #2006627695.*

Endnotes

Material in the Jonathan Booth sidebars, which appear throughout the book, was developed from Kaye Briegel, "Jonathan Booth," in *Signal Hill: An Oral History Collection* (Signal Hill, CA: City of Signal Hill, 1992), 43–89.

Foreword

Epigraph: Alex de Tocqueville, Democracy in America was originally published in French in two volumes, the first in 1825 and the second in 1840, by Saunders and Otley in London. This classic French text was first translated to English by Henry Reeve in 1835 and later revised by Francis Bowen. It was reissued in 1945 in a modern, edited edition by publisher Alfred A. Knopf.

1   Thomas Walker, "Well Abandonment Equivalency Standards," Walker & Evans, Huntington Beach, October 7, 2014, Section 2.1.

Introduction

1   The Historical Society of Southern California's *Southern California Quarterly*, Fall 2015, Volume 97, No. 3 (University of California Press) contains the papers and photographs presented at the April 11, 2015, colloquium held by the Los Angeles Region Planning History Group in Signal Hill.

Chapter I

Epigraph: "Long Beach and Alamitos," *The Land of Sunshine*, Vol. 6, No. 6, May, 1897.

1   Sources for this section include McCawley, *The First Angelinos*, 24–27; Walter A. Tompkins, *The Little Giant of Signal Hill* (Englewood Cliffs, NJ: Prentice-Hall, 1964), 4; and "An Interesting Discovery Made: Stone

Monument Planted by Coast Survey Corps Fifty Years or More Ago," *Long Beach Evening Tribune*, May 2, 1905.

2   Sources for this section include William McCawley, *The First Angelinos* (Banning, CA: Malki Museum Press, 1996), 23–47; https://www.rancho-loscerritos.org/about-hub/history-hub/; and https://www.rancholosa-lamitos.com/history.html, accessed October 2019. There is a fascinating description of the Great Drought of 1862–1865 and how it devastated the ranchos in the *Los Angeles Times*, May 6, 1991.

3   Sources for this section include Washington State University, online research paper, *Japanese American Internment during World War Two: The History of Anti-Japanese Sentiment in America*, 1-3; Syl MacDowell, "Cucumber Patch Becomes America's Richest Town," *Los Angeles Times*, July 6, 1924; and Tim Grobaty, "Back in the good old days of the lemon ranches" *Long Beach Press Telegram*, April 29, 1988.

Chapter II

Epigraph: Kevin Starr, *Material Dreams: Southern California through the 1920s* (New York: Oxford University Press, 1990), 69.

1   Sources for this section include Signal Hill Improvement Company, *Signal Hill: The Most Beautiful Home Site in Southern California*, 1910, promotional brochure. Reprinted in 1964 by Denni Corporation, Wilmington, California. "Denni & Hughes," City of Signal Hill Archives; Starr, *Material Dreams*, 85.

2   US Census Bureau, Long Beach, CA, 1900, 1910, and 1920.

3   Other sources for this section include Spencer Crump, *Ride the Big Red Cars: How the Trolleys Helped Build Southern California* (Los Angeles: Trans-Anglo Books, 1977), 47, 58; Sam Hall Kaplan, *LA Lost and Found: An Architectural History of Southern California* (Santa Monica: Hennessey & Ingalls, 2000), 67; and Sanborn Map Company, Sanborn Fire Insurance Maps, 1920s, Historical Society of Long Beach collection.

4   Signal Hill Improvement Company, *The Most Beautiful Home Site.*

5   Walter A. Case, "Did You Know That...?," *Long Beach Press Telegram*, March 2, 1936.

6   Other sources for this section include William Rintoul, *Drilling through Time: 75 Years with California's Division of Oil and Gas* (Sacramento: State of California, Department of Conservation, Division of Oil and Gas, 1990), 41–51. This book is an invaluable resource on the history of oil in California.

7   Sources for this section include Blake Gumprecht, *The Los Angeles River: Its Life, Death and Possible Rebirth* (Baltimore: Johns Hopkins University Press, 2001), 144–145, 154, 167, 205.

8   Sources for this section include Rintoul, *Drilling through Time*, 1–2, 41–51; *Summary of Operations, California Oil Fields, Annual Report of the State Oil and Gas Supervisor* (San Francisco: State of California, State Mining Bureau, Department of Petroleum and Gas, February, 1922); Piero Scaruffi, A Timeline of Automobile History, accessed October 2019, https://www.scaruffi.com/politics/cars.html; "DMV History," State of California, Department of Motor Vehicles, www.dmv.ca.gov; and Scott L. Bottles, *Los Angeles and the Automobile: The Making of the Modern City* (Berkeley: University of California Press, 1987), 92–93.

Chapter III

Epigraph: Upton Sinclair, *Oil!*, (New York: Albert & Charles Boni, 1927).

1   Sources for this section include Kenny A. Franks and Paul F. Lambert, *Early California Oil: A Photographic History, 1865–1940* (College Station, TX: Texas A&M University Press, 1985); The California State Mining Bureau issued monthly reports on oil field and refining operations. The April 1922 edition of *Summary of Operations, California Oil Fields*, Volume 7, contains an extensive description of the Long Beach Field, Pages 5–22, including detailed notes on the Discovery Well – Alamitos #1; and Kendall Beaton, *Enterprise in Oil: A History of Shell in the United States* (New York: Appleton-Century-Crofts, Inc., 1957), 174–182.

2   Starr, *Material Dreams*, 59–60; and Rintoul, *Drilling through Time*, 44–45.

3   Division of Oil and Gas, *Summary of Oil Field Operations, California Oil Fields, 54th Annual Report of the State Oil and Gas Supervisor* (Sacramento: State of California, 1968), 11.

4   Franks and Lambert, *Early California Oil*, 106–108; and *Signal Hill Leader*, July 30, 1926, 3.

5   *Western Oil News*, January 6, 1922, 2.

6   Sinclair, *Oil!*

7   Rintoul, *Drilling through Time*, 46.

8   Tompkins, *The Little Giant of Signal Hill*, 2.

9   Franks and Lambert, *Early California Oil*, 102–107; and Jules Tygiel, *The Great Los Angeles Swindle* (New York: Oxford University Press, 1994). Tygiel's work is the definitive book on CC Julian and "Julian Pete" (Julian Petroleum Company).

10 *Saturday Evening Post*, December 17, 1927; and Rintoul, *Drilling through Time*, 72.

11 Tompkins, *The Little Giant of Signal Hill*, 7–9, 51–53.

12 *Long Beach Telegram*, January 23, 1922.

13 *Signal Hill Beacon*, October 2, 1925.

14 Wikipedia, s.v., "William Wolfskill," accessed October 2019, https://en.wikipedia.org/wiki/William_Wolfskill.

15 Other sources for this section include Tompkins, *The Little Giant of Signal Hill*, 7–9, 51–53; and "Samuel B. Mosher is Dead at 77, Founder of Signal Oil & Gas Co.," *New York Times*, August 6, 1970.

Chapter IV

Epigraph: MacDowell, "Cucumber Patch Becomes America's Richest Town."

1 Carey McWilliams, *Southern California: An Island on the Land* (Layton, UT: Gibbs Smith, 1946), 57.

2 "Signal Hill, New Dreams Replace Old," *Los Angeles Times*, June 20, 1971.

3 Sources for this section include The National Susan B. Anthony Museum & House, accessed 2016, https://susanb.org; and William Lavender and Mary Lavender, "Suffrages Storm Over Washington D.C. in 1917," Weidner History Network, accessed October 2019, www.history-net.com/nineteenth-amendment.

4 Rebecca Burleson, City of Signal Hill, "Subject: "Jessie Nelson," City of Signal Hill Memorandum, June 18, 2009. This memorandum contains a number of newspaper citations to Jessie Nelson: "Signal Hill has Woman Mayor: Mrs. Jessie Elwin Nelson as First Chief Executive of New City," *Los Angeles Times*, May 3, 1924; MacDowell, "Cucumber Patch Becomes America's Richest Town"; "Woman Mayor of Signal Hill May Quit," *Long Beach Press Telegram*, March 11, 1925; "Signal Hill's Woman Mayor Resigns from Position," *Long Beach Press Telegram*, March 17, 1925; and "Death Takes First Mayor of Hill City," *Long Beach Press Telegram*, August 29, 1929.

5 *Long Beach Press Telegram*, April 29, 1924.

6 "Incorporated Cities," County of Los Angeles, lacounty.gov.

7 Sources for this section include Burleson, City of Signal Hill Memorandum; and MacDowell, "Cucumber Patch Becomes America's Richest Town."

8 *Signal Hill Beacon*, August 28, 1925, 1.

9 *Signal Hill Beacon*, September 25, 1925.

10 *Signal Hill Leader*, August 20, 1926, 1.

11 *Signal Hill Beacon*, October 9, 1925; and City of Signal Hill, 2006 Water Bond Prospectus, 9.

12 *Signal Hill Beacon*, June 26, 1926, 4.

13 Sources for this section also include City of Signal Hill Board of Trustees (City Council) Meeting Minutes for May 1, May 12, June 16, July 7, July 21, July 28, September 10, September 15, September 22, October 6, and October 20, in 1924, and for February 2, February 16, February 25, March 2, and March 20, in 1925.

14 Sources for this section include James Hamilton, "Historical Oil Shocks" (working paper, National Bureau of Economic Research, Department of Economics, University of California, San Diego, February 1, 2011); and Kevin Starr, *Endangered Dreams: The Great Depression in California* (New York: Oxford University Press, 1996) 132.

15 Starr, *Endangered Dreams*, 319–320.

16 Other sources for this section include PRC Services Corporation, *Historic Resources Assessment Report: David Starr Jordan High School*, prepared for Long Beach Unified School District, March 2013, http://lbschoolbonds.net/pdfs/JordanCEQAInitialStudy_AppendixA.pdf, 9–11, 13.

Chapter V

Epigraph: Corey Washington, "Retrospective Presentation Highlights Oil History in Signal Hill, So Cal," *Signal Tribune*, April 17, 2015.

1 Walker, "Well Abandonment Equivalency Standards."

2 Sources for this section include Long Beach Earthquake: 70th Anniversary, Southern California Earthquake Center, accessed 2016, https://www.scec.org/; Report by the Signal Hill Elementary School Librarian, City of Long Beach Library, [no date]; and Bess Wilson, "Open Air Classes Held at Long Beach Schools & School Head Scores False Quake Reports," *Long Beach Press Telegram*, April 3, 1933.

3 Sources for this section include Division of Oil and Gas, *Summary of Oil Field Operations*, 14; and Rintoul, *Drilling through Time*, 89–93.

4 Sources for this section include D. J. Waldie, *Holy Land: A Suburban Memoir* (New York: Buzz Book for St. Martin's Press, 1996), 73–79; City of Signal Hill, General Plan, City Planning Commission, *1962*, 11, 36–37; and Quinto-Budlong Planning, *Signal Hill Urban Design Study*, May 1970.

5 Sources for this section include Division of Oil and Gas, *Summary of Oil Field Operations*, 12–13; and *Signal Hill West Unit Agreement*, Long Beach Field, Los Angeles County, December 1, 1971.

6 Sources for this section include David Slater, Vice President of Signal Hill Petroleum, "History of Shell Oil," interview with the author, March 17, 2015, Signal Hill, California; and History of Shell Oil, accessed October 2019, www.fundinguniverse.com/company-histories/shell-oil-company-history.

Chapter VI

Epigraph: Richard Nixon, "Reorganization Plan No. 3," message to Congress about establishing EPA, July 1970.

1   Linda Lear, "Rachel Carson's Biography," accessed October 2019, https://www.rachelcarson.org/Bio.aspx.

2   Sources for this section include Keith C. Clarke and Jeffrey J. Hemphill, "The Santa Barbara Oil Spill: A Retrospective," *Yearbook of the Association of Pacific Coast Geographers*, vol. 64 (2002), 157–162.

3   Sources for this section include City of Signal Hill, "Never by Chance: A Brief History of Signal Hill," Golden Anniversary, 1974.

4   Sources for this section include Margaret Leslie Davis, *Rivers in the Desert: William Mulholland and the Inventing of Los Angeles* (New York: Harper Collins, 1993), 89–94.

5   Sources for this section include "Solid Waste Disposal in Los Angeles County," Los Angeles Almanac, accessed 2018, www.laalmanac.com; Kat Eschner, "This 1943 'Hellish Cloud' Was the Most Vivid Warning of LA's Smog Problems to Come," *Smithsonian*, July 26, 2017; and South Coast Air Quality Management District [compiler], "The Southland's War on Smog: Fifty Years of Progress Toward Clean Air (through May 1997)," accessed October 2019, https://www.aqmd.gov/home/research/publications/50-years-of-progress.

6   Sources for this section include Chris Haire, "Larry Forester, longtime Signal Hill councilman, will soon step away from public life," *Long Beach Press Telegram*, March 2, 2019; Ken Farfsing and Richard Watson, "Stormwater Funding Options, Providing Sustainable Water Quality Funding in Los Angeles County," May 21, 2014, http://www.scag.ca.gov/committees/committeedoclibrary/eec060514_stormwaterreport.pdf; and Steve Scauzillo, "A moment to capture," *Long Beach Press Telegram*, November 19, 2017.

Chapter VII

Epigraph: Brittany Woolsey. "Signal Hill still booming at 90." *Orange Couny Register*, April 19, 2014.

1   Sources for this section include City of Signal Hill Ordinance No. 74-7-729, July 16, 1974.

2   Sources for this section include "History of Shell Oil," interview with Slater; accessed October 2019, www.fundinguniverse.com/company-histories/shell-oil-company-history; and accessed October 2019, http://www.shpi.net/about-us/our-history.aspx.

3   Claudine Burnett, "A look at bygone days," *Signal Hill Tribune*, June 15, 2018; "1920s Fight Club in downtown Huntington Beach," Historic

Huntington Beach, June 28, 2017, http://historichuntingtonbeach.blog-spot.com/2017/06/1920s-fight-club-in-downtown-huntington.html.

4   "Broadcasting and Music on the Hill—Signal Hill, CA," accessed October, 2019, https://www.waymarking.com/waymarks/WMQX1E_Broadcasting_and_Music_on_the_Hill_Signal_Hill_CA.

5   "Farewell, Foothill," *Orange County Weekly*, July 27, 2000; and "Obituary, Bonnie Price," *Long Beach Press Telegram*, December 23, 2008.

6   "Eastman Signs Lease at Signal Hill Center," *Los Angeles Times*, May 18, 1986.

7   Peter Eisner, "Sol Price, 93, father of warehouse superstores," *Washington Post*, December 15, 2009.

8   Scott, Lehrer, "Battle Continues Over Price Club," *Los Angeles Times*, July 28, 1985; and Phillip Zokel, "Long-Time Signal Hill councilman Louis Dare dies at 94," *Long Beach Press Telegram*, February 19, 2014.

9   Bottles, *Los Angeles and the Automobile*, 211, 217–218.

10   Marilyn Cenovich, "The Story of Cerritos: A History in Progress," City of Cerritos, 1995, accessed October 2019, chapters 8 and 9, http://menu.ci.cerritos.ca.us/collections/local_history/cl_lhStory.htm.

11   Sources for this section include Signal Hill Redevelopment Agency, Project No. 1. Tax Allocation Series 1985, Final Opinion from Morrison & Forester, Tax Allocation Bond of December 23, 1985; There is a good history of the former redevelopment agency in RDA staff reports dated January 20, 2009, June 5, 2010, March 4, 2011, and March 20, 2011, as the RDA approved and implemented a $24 million land purchasing program focusing on distressed properties; James Rainey, "Signal Hill Auto Center Mired in Past," *Los Angeles Times*, August 1990; Erika Engle, "Mike Salta, longtime Hawaii auto dealer dies," *Star Advertiser*, July 8, 2014; Wikipedia, s.v., "Blue Line (Los Angeles Metro)," last modified November 19, 2019, https://en.wikipedia.org/wiki/Blue_Line_(Los_Angeles_Metro); and Nancy Wride, "Rebirth of Signal Hill," *Los Angeles Times*, January 7, 2002.

12   Wikipedia, s.v., "2005 California special election," last modified September 9, 2019, https://en.wikipedia.org/wiki/2005_California_special_election.

13   Sean Belk, "Signal Hill's new police station opens to serve community 'well into the next century,'" *Signal Hill Tribune*, February 1, 2013.

14   Susan Orlean, *The Library Book* (New York: Simon and Schuster, 2018), 130–131.

15   Phillip Zonkel, "Signal Hill library celebrates 85 years," *Long Beach Press Telegram*, December 17, 2013.

16 Samantha Mehlinger, "Mayor Tina Hansen on Signal Hill's Momentum, Business Focus," *Long Beach Business Journal*, August 27, 2018.

17 John Woolfolk Tseipel, "Jerry Brown's talk of ending redevelopment sparks fears, cheers around California," *East Bay Times*, January 5, 2011.

18 Sources for this section include Sean Belk, "Signal Hill City Officials vow to fight for RDA bond money to construct new library," *Signal Hill Tribune*, October 4, 2013; and Anita W. Harris, "SH City Council approves contracts for new library," *Signal Hill Tribune*, January 12, 2018.

Chapter VIII

Epigraph: City of Signal Hill, "2013–2021 Housing Element of the General Plan, Adopted by City Council February 4, 2014," accessed October 2019, https://www.cityofsignalhill.org/DocumentCenter/View/2238/Signal-Hill-2013-2021-HE-2-6-14?bidId.

1 Staff report, Gary Jones, Directory of Community Development, City of Signal Hill, Sept 7, 2010.

2 City of Signal Hill, Hilltop Specific Plan, November 5, 1993.

3 City of Signal Hill, California Crown Specific Plan Area 5, October 1990.

4 City of Signal Hill, Water Bond, 2006, Page 10.

5 City of Signal Hill, SP-11 Crescent Heights Historic District Specific Plan; "Signal Hill Council signs off on 'Crescent Square' residential specific plan at brief meeting," *Signal Hill Tribune*, September 19, 2014; and Amanda Briney, "The Importance of Historic Preservation," The Thought Company, April 10, 2019.

6 Sources for this section include Wikipedia, s.v., "California Geological Survey," accessed November 2019, last modified September 9, 2019, https://en.wikipedia.org/wiki/California_Geological_Survey; *Summary of Operations, California Oil Fields* (San Francisco: State of California, State Mining Bureau, Department of Petroleum and Gas, July, 1921), 28–30; accessed November 2019, https://www.conservation.ca.gov/calgem/Pages/Oil-and-Gas.aspx; and SESPE Consulting, Inc., *CEQA Initial Study Signal Hill Oil Code Amendment*, report prepared for the City of Signal Hill, April 2015, 6–12, http://cityofsignalhill.granicus.com/MetaViewer.php?view_id=2&clip_id=931&meta_id=46616.

7 "Signal Hill to host opening of its first dog park," *Signal Hill Tribune*, March 15, 2018

8 Starr, *Material Dreams*, 86.

9 Angelo Verzoni, "The day that shook L.A., The Long Beach Earthquake of 1933," *NEPA Journal*, March 2018.

10 Molly Hennessy-Fiske, "1933 Long Beach temblor defined Southern California as 'earthquake county,'" *Los Angeles Times*, March 10, 2008.

11 Historical Population Data for California, State of California, Department of Finance. http://www.dof.ca.gov/Forecasting/Demographics/

12 Sources for this section include Brian Addison, "A History of Housing Practices in Long Beach," September 13, 2017, https://www.kcet.org/shows/city-rising/a-history-of-housing-practices-in-long-beach.

13 Sources for this section include Nick Diamantides, "SH celebrates opening of Las Brisas II housing," *Signal Hill Tribune*, October 4, 2007; City of Signal Hill, "2013–2021 Housing Element of the *General Plan*; and Brian Addison, "Signal Hill's New Affordable Housing Community," *Long Beach Post*, September 5, 2014.

Appendix

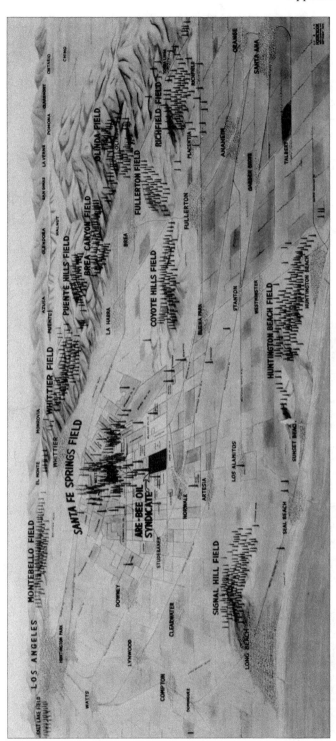

View of oil fields around Los Angeles, 1922. (US Library of Congress, public domain.)

View of oil fields around Los Angeles, 1922. (US Library of Congress, public domain.)

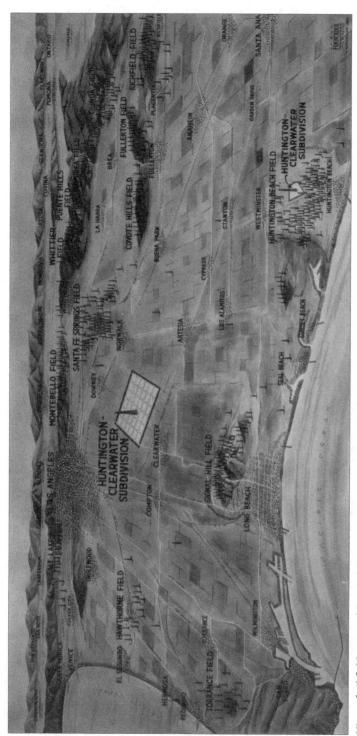

View of oil fields around Los Angeles, 1922. (US Library of Congress, public domain.)

Index

Photographs and illustrations are indicated by an italicized page number.

About the Author

Mr. Farfsing has over forty years of experience in city management, community development, redevelopment, and economic development from working in six Southern California communities. He served as Signal Hill's city manager from 1996 to 2015. Ken also served as the city manager for South Pasadena (1991–1996) and for Carson (2015–2018).

Prior to managing these cities, he served as an assistant city manager for the City of Downey (1988–1991) and worked in various city planning capacities for the City of La Verne (1981–1988), including as the director of community development. Ken obtained his BA in history from the University of California at Berkeley in 1976. He received his master's degree in urban planning from the University of Southern California in 1980. He was the planning intern for the City of Santa Fe Springs (1979–1981).

Ken has always had a respect for history and the lessons that we can learn from it. In October 2014, he co-authored "Stormwater Funding Options: Providing Sustainable Water Quality Funding in Los Angeles County." This report included an extensive historical review of water and flood control issues in Los Angeles County. The report led the way to the successful passage of a property tax measure in 2018 geared towards capturing and reusing stormwater in the county. As a board member of the Los Angeles Region Planning History Group, he helped organize their 2015 Colloquium XI, "Black Gold in Paradise."

Ken retired from local government service in 2018, which has allowed him the time to pursue other interests, including completing this book. He is currently organizing a program to explore the historical roots and solutions to the region's chronic housing crisis.